Mervyn Peake
The Man and His Art

COMPILED BY SEBASTIAN PEAKE AND ALISON ELDRED
EDITED BY G. PETER WINNINGTON

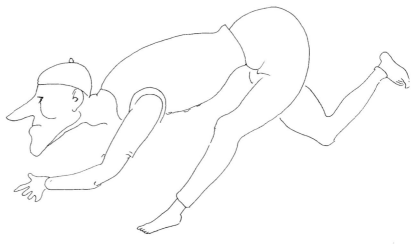

Peter Owen Publishers

London and Chester Springs

To the memory of Mervyn Peake
and Maeve Gilmore

PETER OWEN PUBLISHERS
73 Kenway Road
London sw5 0RE

Peter Owen books are distributed in the USA by
Dufour Editions Inc., Chester Springs, PA 19425-0007

First published in Great Britain by Peter Owen Publishers 2006

ISBN 0 7206 1284 5

A catalogue record for this book is available from the British Library

Designed by Benedict Richards
Printed and bound by Excel Print Media Pte Ltd, Singapore

Acknowledgements

The source of images not owned by the Peake Estate is printed beside the respective illustrations. We wish to express our especial gratitude to Chris Beetles who generously granted us free use of a great many images; without them this book would have been far less comprehensive. Other persons have waived their right to be identified as the owners. Andy Wilson, on behalf of the team he directed on the BBC *Gormenghast*, has kindly allowed us to reproduce some of the storyboards prepared for the adaptation.

We wish to thank the Estate of Bill Brandt for permission to reproduce his photograph of Peake (on p. 18); the Estate of Walter de la Mare, administered by the Society of Authors, for permission to quote from 'Peacock Pie'; the Folio Society for an extract from Michael Moorcock's Introduction to their illustrated edition of *Titus Groan* (1992) as well as images from both *Droll Stories* by Balzac and Stevenson's *Dr Jekyll and Mr Hyde*; and John Vernon Lord for permission to quote from his contribution to *Picture This: The Artist as Illustrator* edited by Sylvia Backemeyer, A. and C. Black, 2005.

IMAGE COURTESY OF CHRIS BEETLES GALLERY

If I could see, not surfaces,
But could express
What lies beneath the skin
Where the blood moves
In fruit or head or stone,
Then would I know the one
Essential
And my eyes
When dead
Would give the worm
No hollow food.

If I could feel
My words of wax were struck

By the rare seal
Of crested truth,
Then would I give bold birth
To long
Rivers of song.

Where is that inexhaustible,
That secret genesis
Of Sound and Sight?
It is too close for me,
It lies
Unexcavated by these eyes
In the lost archives of my heart.

Mervyn Peake

Preface

SEBASTIAN PEAKE

Sixty years on, the world of Titus Groan and his castle remains as contemporary as when it was first published in 1946. It is generally accepted that the Gormenghast trilogy offers one of the most original flights of imaginative writing of the twentieth century, and Mervyn Peake is best remembered for this timeless and highly influential work.

Less well known, however, is my father's prolific output as a painter, a writer of children's books and nonsense verse, war artist and poet and the illustrations and drawings he produced for such classic texts as *Treasure Island*, *Alice in Wonderland*, *The Rime of the Ancient Mariner* and *Household Tales* by the brothers Grimm. This book aims to correct the imbalance between his rightful place as a unique writer and that as an artist excelling in many other fields. On learning that a new book on the art of Mervyn Peake was in preparation, several writers and artists were eager to contribute, the main reason cited for their enthusiastic willingness being his profound and lasting influence on their own work.

The wonderfully inspired Michael Moorcock, for instance, has remained a principal champion of my father's work all his life and has taken every opportunity to promote his work. For his role as enthusiast and persuader, resulting in the reissue in 1970 of the trilogy by Penguin Books as a Modern Classic, Mike will always be remembered with deep gratitude by the Peake family. In this volume he expresses his admiration for a writer who inspired him and pays homage to my mother, Maeve Gilmore, who befriended him.

Langdon Jones, musician, writer and friend of Michael Moorcock, tells how he spent a year meticulously comparing the various versions of the original manuscripts of *Titus Alone* and presented Penguin with a text much closer to that which the author had originally intended. It is this edition that is in print today.

John Wood was an ardent student of my father's at the Central School of Art. He visited our home at Wallington and introduced me to the ratamacue, paradiddle, ruff and double stroke roll on the drums. He has contributed his memories of my father's teaching.

Above
Mervyn Peake with his two sons, photographed by Raymond Kleboe for the *Picture Post* in 1946

Frontispiece (page 2)
Mervyn Peake at Wallington, early 1930s

Top left
Sebastian and Fabian as clowns on
Sark, 1948

Top right
Sebastian drawn in black chalk,
c. 1951

Above
The Peake family in the garden at
Smarden, summer 1951

Fiction writers readily acknowledge the impact of the Titus books, as they understand the vital connection between the way the characters come alive and the fundamentally visual way in which they are described. Joanne Harris, one of whose many novels, *Chocolat*, was not only highly successful but also made into a film and shown internationally, writes of how Gormenghast has affected her writing.

Many of today's generation of illustrators recognize the influence of my father's work on their own. John Howe, the artist and book illustrator, describes the effect it had on him as a teenager, and its consequences in his own life, while Chris Riddell, the cartoonist and illustrator, comments on my father's approach to drawing as expressed in *The Craft of the Lead Pencil*, which was published in 1946, the same year as *Titus Groan*.

The Titus books have also inspired adaptations for the theatre and television. Among them, David Glass's powerfully minimalist rendering of the story has amazed audiences not only in Britain but across the world. Estelle Daniel displayed unparalleled tenacity during the five years it took her to bring a four-part BBC television series to the screen when at times it looked as though the whole project might have to be abandoned. But my father's own plays remain a little-known province of his art. Here the characters of his best-known play, *The Wit to Woo*, come alive in his vivid and lively sketches.

When the idea of a new book on my father's life and artistic imagination was suggested by Peter Owen, I approached Peter Winnington to act as editor, for his knowledge of my father's *œuvre* is unmatched, and I am glad to say that he accepted

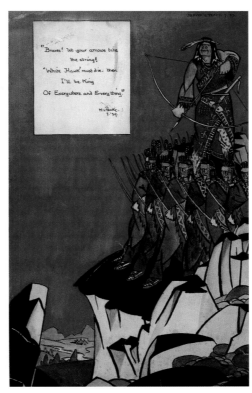

the daunting task of interweaving a narrative around the eclectic mix of painting, poetry, illustration and writing which made up my father's world.

For more than thirty years now Peter has edited bi-annual periodicals, first *The Mervyn Peake Review* and now *Peake Studies*, adding greatly to the recognition of my father's work through well-chosen articles by academics and admirers alike. He understands both the heart of his subject and the mind that drove it and has worked assiduously to unravel the history, dynamic and cultural influences that produced this unique, multi-talented artist, first in a biography (published by Peter Owen in 2000) and now in a forthcoming critical study. But Peter has had a tough job on his hands, for there is no easy answer, certainly no rational explanation, for the appearance of an exceptional talent; it occurs every once in a while to beguile us and gasp at, while leaving the observer essentially mute in the presence of this *embarras de richesse*.

The introduction to my other collaborator on this book was simple. 'This is Alison,' announced Chris Beetles, the gallery owner. 'She has just bought one of your father's drawings from *Witchcraft in England*.' So began a friendship which has had the life and work of my father at its core. Ideas flowed from Alison, an established and respected artists' agent, from that very first moment and have continued, often on a daily basis, for the past seven years. The culmination of this mutual effort to present the public with an up-to-date reassessment of Mervyn Peake's art, using as many unpublished drawings and paintings as possible, is almost entirely due to Alison's love of his painting and illustration. Without her unflagging desire to see this happen, it might well have remained just an idea.

Above left
Sebastian in the clown costume designed by his father for the Sark Fête, 1948

Above right
Indian braves; a drawing and short poem, 1929

Contents

Introduction

MICHAEL MOORCOCK

People who didn't know him very well used to say Mervyn Peake's books were so darkly complex that writing them had sent him mad. Others who knew him a little better understood how cleverly Peake had formalized his own experience and observations. He was one of the most deeply sane individuals you could hope to meet. He was a conscious artist, with a wicked wit and a tremendous love of life. 'He has magic in his pen,' said Charles Morgan. 'He can annihilate the dimensions.'

Anthony Burgess thought the English mistrusted Peake for being too talented. He was a first-class illustrator (at one time 'the most fashionable in England', according to Quentin Crisp), a fine poet and an outstanding painter. His novels, said Burgess, are 'aggressively three-dimensional . . . showing the poet as well as the draughtsman . . . It is difficult in post-war English fiction to get away with big rhetorical gestures. Peake manages it because, with him, grandiloquence never means diffuseness; there is no musical emptiness in the most romantic of his descriptions. He is always exact . . . [*Titus Groan*] remains essentially a work of the closed imagination, in which a world parallel to our own is presented in almost paranoiac denseness of detail. But the madness is illusory, and control never falters. It is, if you like, a rich wine of fancy chilled by the intellect to just the right temperature. There is no really close relative to it in all our prose literature. It is uniquely brilliant.'

His wife Maeve's memoir, *A World Away,* is full of stories of scratching the backs of elephants through floorboards to try to keep them quiet while he was sleeping above them, his spontaneous acts of romantic generosity, his dashing gestures and glorious sense of fun, his willingness to give drawings or poems away to anyone who said they liked them, his London expeditions, drawing faces from Soho, Limehouse, Wapping – what he called 'head-hunting'. He courted her elegantly and with humour. He was, she said, 'unique, dark and majestic'. Tea at Lyons Corner House, a trip on a tram, and she was his for ever. He was conscripted in the Second World War, was in London a great deal during the Blitz and

On page 10
Mervyn Peake reading in the garden at Wallington in the 1930s

Above
Mervyn Peake drawing in Wiesbaden, Germany, May 1945

A wash drawing of Maeve drying
her hair, 1940s

witnessed the horrors of Belsen soon after it was liberated, producing studies that are remarkable for their humanity and sympathy, experience he used in his last book. He, like most of us, somehow stayed roughly sane, if a little overwrought, throughout the war. His practical jokes, often concocted with Graham Greene, were elaborate and subtle.

Mervyn Peake was inspiring, joyful company whose tragedy was not in his life or work but in whatever ill luck cursed him with Parkinson's disease. 'If we went out,' said Maeve, 'it often seemed that he was drunk or drugged, and offence would be taken. I longed to shelter him and resented the intelligent ones who turned their backs on him. It's very painful to see such a gentle man cold-shouldered.' Increasingly unable to draw, or work on the fourth Titus book, he was, by the mid-1960s, institutionalized and in the last stages of his illness. His public reputation had vanished. Neither Greene, Bowen nor Burgess, all of them admirers, had enough influence to convince his publishers to return his books to print.

If there is an unsung hero of Mervyn Peake's life and career it has to be Oliver Caldecott, painter and publisher, who became head of the Penguin fiction list, founded Wildwood House and died prematurely. Ollie and Moira Caldecott, South African exiles, had been friends of mine for several years and we shared a mutual enthusiasm for the Gormenghast sequence. We had made earlier efforts to persuade someone to reprint it, but as usual were told there was no readership for the books. Caldecott wouldn't give up hope.

I had been instrumental in getting a couple of Mervyn's short stories published and ran some fragments of fiction, poetry and drawings in my magazine *New Worlds*. Some of his poetry was still in print, together with one or two illustrated books, but he was thoroughly out of fashion, his reputation not helped by Kingsley Amis describing him as 'a bad fantasy writer of maverick status', revealing a tendency for those who trawled the margins to link him with the authors of horror stories and talking-animal books.

Peake spoke of his artistic experiments as 'the smashing of another window pane'. He wasn't looking for reassurance. He was looking for truth. A fascinated explorer of human personality, a confronter of realities, beaming his brilliance here and there into our common darkness, a narrative genius able to control a vast range of characters (no more grotesque than life and many of them wonderfully comic), Peake told a complex narrative, much of which is based upon the ambitions of a single, determined individual, Steerpike, whose rise from the depths of society (or 'Gormenghast' as it is called) and extraordinary climb and fall has a monumental, Dickensian quality which keeps you reading at fever pitch; the stuff of solid, grown-up full-strength fiction. Real experience, freshly described. 'It's not so much their blindness', he said of his more conventional contemporaries, 'as their love of blinkers that spells stagnation.' *Gormenghast* was written by a real poet, with a real relish for words and a real feel for the alienated, a painter who could see the extraordinary beneath the apparently

Above
The dust-jackets designed by Mervyn Peake for the first editions of the Titus books

Above
Muzzlehatch the lover of animals.
A drawing for *Titus Alone*, 1959

nondescript. Closer to the best Zola than any of the generic tosh which was published in the 1970s.

In his introduction to the first collection of his drawings Peake wrote, 'After all, there are no rules. With the wealth, skill, daring, vision of many centuries at one's back, yet one is ultimately quite alone. For it is one's ambition to create one's own world in a style germane to its substance, and to people it with its native forms and denizens that never were before, yet have their roots in one's experience. As the earth was thrown from the sun, so from the earth the artist must fling out into space, complete from pole to pole, his own world which, whatsoever form it takes, is the colour of the globe it flew from, as the world itself is coloured by the sun.'

Born in China, still carrying a feel of the exotic about him, a fine painter, illustrator, poet and novelist, Peake was a sunny, buoyant source of life for so many who knew him. His optimism could be unrealistic, but he was never short of it. He was charming and attractive, generous and expansive by nature, combining his dark

IMAGE COURTESY OF UNIVERSITY COLLEGE LONDON

IMAGE COURTESY OF UNIVERSITY COLLEGE LONDON

Celtic good looks with a fine sense of style. Although he'd always supported his family, he'd never had much of a knack for making money – he received five pounds for the entire set of illustrations to *The Hunting of the Snark*. He wasn't much good at anticipating bills; only as his illness worsened did his anxieties begin to get a grip on him, and he had exaggerated hopes for his surreal play, *The Wit to Woo*, which failed badly.

Knowing little of the brain in those days – this was before Alzheimer's or Parkinson's diseases were understood – we watched helplessly as Mervyn declined into some mysterious form of dementia, while the surgeons hacked at his frontal lobes and further destroyed his ability to work and reason. The frustration was terrible. His instinctive intelligence, his kindness, even his wit flickered in his eyes but were all trapped, inexpressible. 'It feels like everything's being stolen,' he said once to me. Here was an extraordinary man, his head a treasure-house of invention, poetry, characters, ideas, being destroyed from within while his genius was rejected by the literary and art world of the day.

When art critics of reputation such as Edwin Mullins tried to write about Peake, editors would turn the idea down. I had only modest success, mostly in low-circulation literary magazines and fanzines. The story, even then, was that Peake had lost his mind through the strain of writing such dark books. All the fictional madness he had created had caught up with him. That story was damaging, sensational nonsense recklessly perpetuated by Quentin Crisp ('all that darkness, dear, gets to you in the end'), for whom Peake had once illustrated a small book and to whom the Peakes had been consistently kind in the years before his notoriety.

The last novel of the sequence, *Titus Alone*, did indeed contain structural weaknesses which we had all assumed were Mervyn's as his control of his work became shaky. Then, one afternoon, Langdon Jones, composer of a superb musical setting for Peake's narrative poem of the Blitz, *The Rhyme of the Flying Bomb*, was leafing through the manuscript books of the novel, which Maeve Peake had shown him,

Above left

Titus rides out beyond the castle walls, a sketch from the manuscript of *Gormenghast*

Above right

Irma Prunesquallor sitting 'with her pelvis at least a foot to the rear of an excited perpendicular – her thorax, neck and head' (*Titus Groan*, p. 304); a sketch from the manuscript

Above

Mervyn Peake photographed in his
Soho flat by Bill Brandt, 1943

when he realized that much of what was missing from the published book was actually in the manuscript. Checking further, he found that the book had been very badly edited by a third party, with whole characters and scenes cut. His account of how he restored the text is printed later in this volume.

Jones worked on *Titus Alone* for over a year, and when he had finished we suggested to the original publishers that they should reissue the book with the new version of the text. Not only did they not want to publish any of the books; they were anxious to hide the fact that the last one had been so badly butchered. They became distinctly negative about the whole thing. I proposed to Maeve that we begin the process of buying back the rights. Meanwhile Mervyn became increasingly unwell.

One day Oliver Caldecott said mysteriously that he was hoping to get a new job that might make things a bit easier. And then he phoned to tell me, with considerable glee, that he was now 'the guy who picks the Penguins'. And, of course, our first action must be to sort out the Gormenghast books and decide how to get them back into print.

Needless to say, the moment Penguin showed interest, the original publisher saw a new value in the books. They were happy to lease the paperback rights. They were still very reluctant to undertake a new edition of *Titus Alone,* however. Eventually the whole production was taken over by Oliver, whose idea it was to illustrate all three novels with drawings from Mervyn's own notebooks. The text of the last, *Titus Alone,* was restored. The beautiful new hardbacks were bound versions of the characteristic Penguin editions. Anthony Burgess gladly contributed an introduction to *Titus Groan,* which he believed to be a masterpiece, and Oliver brought the three volumes out as Penguin Modern Classics. It was the perfect way to publish the books, boldly, enthusiastically and unapologetically, in the best possible editions Mervyn could have.

Next, with the considerable help of my ex-wife Hilary Bailey, Maeve Peake was persuaded to write her wonderful memoir of Mervyn, *A World Away,* which Giles Gordon, another Peake fan, then at Gollancz, was delighted to publish – 'the most touching book I've ever read', he said. And BBC's 'Monitor' series began production of its rather gothic television programme on Peake. He was getting a new, appreciative public. Too late, unfortunately, for him to realize it. I remember going with Maeve to the Priory at Roehampton to take him some of the publicity for the new editions, to show him that his books were to be republished and what they would look like. He nodded blankly, mumbled something and lowered his eyes. It was almost as if he could not himself bear the irony. Maeve and his children had to deal with many similar moments.

The rest is more or less history. A history spotted with bad media features about Mervyn that insist on perpetuating his story as a doomed loony. Bill Brandt showed him as a glowering Celt, a sort of unsodden Dylan Thomas, and his romantic good looks help project this image. Women certainly fell in love with his sheer beauty.

And then with his charm. And then with his wit. And then they were lost. After he married Maeve, Peake's home life was about as ordinary and chaotic as the usual bohemian family's. Their mutual love was remarkable, as was the passion and enthusiasm of the whole wonderful tribe. As he faded into the final stages of his disease we were all overwhelmed by an ongoing sense of loss, of disbelief, as if the sun itself were going out.

Peake was neither a saint nor a satanic presence, and what was so marvellous for me, when I first went to see him as a boy, was realizing that so much rich talent could come from such a graceful, pleasant, rather modest man who lived in a suburban house much like mine. He was amused by my enthusiasm. I was in no doubt, though, that I had met my first authentic genius.

In time, of course, many others have come to share that view, until eventually nearly all Peake's work is back in print, new editions of his stories and poems have been produced, public exhibitions have presented his drawings and paintings, and various dramatic versions of his novels have been produced, all the way from the lavish adaptation by the BBC in 2000 to the extraordinary minimalist version of *Gormenghast* by David Glass, not forgetting the Derek Jacobi television version of the charming short novel *Mr Pye*.

Peake had a huge, romantic imagination, a Welsh eloquence and a wry, affectionate wit. His technical mastery, both of narrative and line, remains unmatched. 'To be a good classicist', he said, 'you must cultivate romance. To be a good romantic, you must steep yourself in classicism.' He was both an heir to the great Victorians and a precursor to the postmodernists and the magic realists. His statements frequently anticipated the likes of Salman Rushdie. He influenced a generation of authors, among them Angela Carter, Peter Ackroyd and the two Iains, Sinclair and Banks, who found that it was possible to write imaginatively and inventively about character and real experience while setting their stories in subtly unfamiliar worlds.

Peake's own attitude is best summed up by a poem that achieved popularity some forty years after he wrote it. 'To live at all', he said, 'is miracle enough.' Of course he did much more than live. 'Art', he used to say, 'is ultimately sorcery.' He infused life and art into everything he touched. And his sorceries continue to entrance us.

Scene outside Peking.

Outside city wall. Peking.

1 A Chinese Childhood

SEBASTIAN PEAKE

Box within a box, like a Chinese puzzle – so it seems to me, my Chinese childhood –
and only half do I believe in those faraway days, lost in the black and engulfing sea.

Mervyn Peake

Straight after graduating in medicine from Edinburgh University in 1898 my grandfather, Ernest Cromwell Peake, known to the family as 'Doc', offered his services to the London Missionary Society. He was posted to China, and after a six-week boat journey from England he sailed up the Yangtse from Shanghai to Yo-Chow (*Yueyang* in Pinyin). There he worked with other missionary doctors for a couple of years while learning Chinese. Then he proceeded into the heart of Hunan province, an area as yet closed to the outside world and a further six-week journey up the Hsing river. When he and a colleague set up their mission early in 1902 they were the sole Europeans in Hengchow (*Hengyang*), a city of some 250,000 inhabitants.

These river journeys made a deep impression on Doc, and in his memoir, written almost fifty years later, he left vivid descriptions of them. The junk that he chartered had large painted eyes that it might clearly see its way, but it was the skill of the captain, the 'old plank' in Chinese, that kept them off the treacherous rocks and sandbanks. At one point a severe storm obliged them to take refuge in a creek for several days. Whenever the wind failed the crew resorted to poling – punting on a large scale – or else hired shore-based 'trackers' to haul the vessel upstream.

When Doc ventured into a riverside village he met none of the rudeness he had been told to expect. These rural Chinese had never seen a 'Western barbarian' before. The men making furrows with wooden ploughs drawn by water-buffalo and the women kneeling on the riverbank to wash clothes were curious but not unfriendly. A man fishing with a cormorant reacted with wide-eyed amazement when he realized that Doc was watching him and responded to his polite salutation 'Have you had your rice?' with a wide grin.

It was otherwise when Doc reached Hengchow. A crowd gathered in silent stupefaction as he disembarked, and then shouts of 'Kill the foreign devil' could be heard from the rear and clods of earth were flung. Thanks to the boatmen, he reached an inn unharmed. 'The doors were bolted behind us, and the crowd, after

Facing page, top
Bathing outside Peking,
photographed by Dr Peake

Bottom
Camels in front of the south-east
watch-tower in the city wall of
Peking, photographed by Dr Peake

Above
Dr Peake (second from the left in
the back row) with fellow medical
missionaries, Hankow, 1907

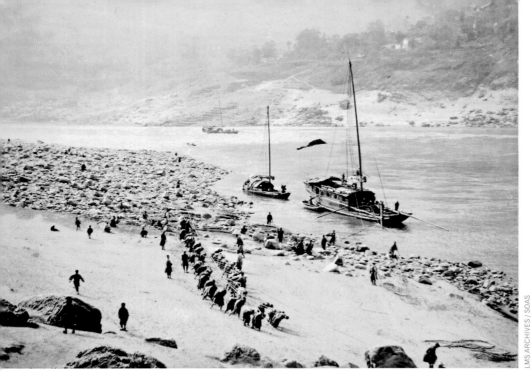

Top left
'Trackers' at work on the Yangtse river

Top right
Water-buffalo ploughing

Above
Chinaman with fish; a pen-and-ink drawing from the manuscript of *Gormenghast*

a noisy demonstration in the street, finally dispersed.' For months he could not venture into the street without attracting a disorderly throng who would press around him. His blue eyes amazed them. 'Cats' eyes!' they would shout, and then 'No pigtail! And look at his outlandish clothes!'

To explore the town, he purchased his own sedan chair and hired bearers.

Having a latticed-curtain to let down, I was able to see without being observed. In this way I acquired a good idea of the city and of its wide extent.

The tortuous streets, not more than ten feet in width, seemed always to be over-crowded and thick with the peculiar odour of spices and stale sweat. They were paved with stone, and down both sides of the roadway ran open sewers, whose odour permeated the atmosphere. The shops, without doors or glass fronts, opened directly on to the streets; a paving stone across the noisome drains functioned as a bridge for customers.

I was struck by the number of street hawkers and by the variety of the wares which they carried suspended from the extremities of their bamboo poles. There were baskets, brushes, bundles of firewood, paper lanterns, palm-leaf fans, live fish and eels in tubs, goldfish, vegetables, melons and dates, edible bamboo shoots and lotus-lily seeds, peanuts, sweets and cakes, eggs, and even water for sale.

Seated at the roadside there were letter-writers, story-tellers, puppet shows, barbers shaving heads, and travelling cooks serving tasty bits from their portable stoves, with semi-naked children and mangy dogs sniffing around them.

Blue predominated in the garments of both men and women; and gold was everywhere in the gilded hieroglyphics inscribed on the vertical shop signs suspended over the heads of the people. The men wore long loose gowns; some of silk but most of cotton. The sweating coolies were content to be as nature made them, except for a loin-cloth of cotton and sandals of plaited straw. The women, not many of whom were to be seen, wore very wide brightly coloured trousers, surmounted by loose tunics. They were contending against great odds in making their way through the turbulent crowd, and their difficulties were greatly increased by the fact that, owing to the pernicious custom of foot-binding, they could only hobble in a stiff and ungainly manner.

Gaining the confidence of the local people took time, but eventually he set up a rudimentary practice, and patients, intimidated and hesitant at first, began seeking his medical advice. Further integration came after a successful cataract operation on a local scholar. With his sight restored, the good man sought out the blind and brought them in a long file to the surgery, each holding the pigtail of the man in front. Doc's services were in increasing demand.

Each summer the European missionaries in central China retreated from the heat of the plains to the heights of Kuling. In his memoir Doc recalls how, after the five- or six-day journey down the Hsing river and then the Yangtse, bearers with palanquins would be waiting for them at Kiukiang (*Jiujiang*).

The first ten or twelve miles crossed flat country bordering the river. It was very hot and steamy as we wound our way in and out between the rice fields. The rice, standing in several inches of water, was well grown and of a lovely green. Innumerable frogs croaked in its cool shade, and there were herons, looking strikingly in harmony with their environment and thoroughly contented with their feeding ground. Now and again we passed through tiny villages, where our chairs would be unceremoniously dumped down among the pigs and chickens. This gave us an

Top
Porters carrying a missionary in a sedan chair

Right
The missionaries' villas at Kuling, photographed by Dr Peake, *c.* 1905

Top left
Bearers with palanquins climbing the steps up to Kuling from the plain

Centre
Looking down from Kuling at the Yangtse

Right
Steamer flying the Red Cross flag during fighting between the Imperialists and the Revolutionaries, Hankow, 1911

Above
The dead on the banks of the Yangtse near Hankow, photographed by Dr Peake in 1911

opportunity to stretch our legs, while our sweating coolies imbibed copious draughts of tea. By midday we had reached the Rest House in the foothills, a picturesque wooden building ensconced in a bamboo grove.

After lunch a fresh team of bearers attacked the ascent of the steep mountainside, climbing 3,500 feet in five miles. Roughly laid stone steps, 3 or 4 feet wide, formed a good track all the way up. The bearers were very sure-footed, but from time to time, when the steepness made it feel as though the palanquin were tilted on end, I preferred to climb on foot. It was hard going, but there was ample compensation in the wild scenery: deep glens, turbulent streams, and waterfalls. Clumps of bamboo, 50 to 40 feet in height, clothed many of the slopes, and in among the tall grasses were magnificent specimens of red and white tiger-lilies and trumpet lilies.

In the evening we reached our bungalow, one of several that the various Missions have disposed irregularly up the mountain slopes. Far below we could catch glimpses of the narrow path by which we had ascended and, beyond the green paddyfields of the plain, the broad Yangtse-Kiang. That night, for the first time for months, we slept under blankets, and without mosquito nets.

It was up at Kuling that Doc met his wife, my grandmother Beth, who was on leave from the Hong Kong mission. And it also up at Kuling that my father Mervyn was born in July 1911. That summer, fighting broke out as the south of China threw off the Manchurian dynasty that had oppressed it for so long and became a republic under President Sun Yat-sen. The formal resignation of the Boy-Emperor took place early in 1912.

While my grandmother remained up at Kuling with little Mervyn Doc joined the few doctors in Hankow (*Hankou*) who were organizing aid to the wounded under the Red Cross. As they approached the city the dead were still lying on the riverbank just as they had fallen. After several days treating the people of Hankow he was loaned a steam launch to rescue the wounded from a dressing station further upstream. On his second trip they were picking up casualties from the waterside when 'bullets began to kick up the dust around us and we felt it wise to leave at once. In spite of our Red Cross flag, we were fired on from across the water. [It is quite possible that in 1911 Chinese conscripts were unaware of the significance of the flag.] One shell pierced the superstructure . . . but we reached the British Settlement in safety.'

Soon after peace returned Doc was sent to take charge of the MacKenzie Memorial Hospital in Tientsin (*Tianjin*), eight hundred miles to the north. The city already had a population of over a million Chinese crowded within its narrow streets, plus large foreign Concessions. It was a major port, although the North River was 'a mere stream when compared with the Yangtse but deep enough for foreign vessels coming in on the tide'. The hospital compound in the French Concession was to be their family home until the end of 1922, when they returned to England. For ten years Doc worked very hard, restoring the hospital buildings, training staff and, with the help of my grandmother, who served as matron, treating tens of thousands of patients. As suggested in my father's juvenile 'Letter from China' much of the work was surgical, for the Chinese of Tientsin had great faith in the curative power of the Westerners' scalpel.

In the compound there were six grey-stone houses for the staff, all in a line, and in my father's memory they looked 'as though they had been flown over from Croydon'. He lived in the fourth, at the tennis-court end, and he 'loved that great grey house with two verandas, upstairs and down'. The compound where he played was his world, his 'arena', 'a world surrounded by a wall. And on the other side of the wall was China.' In one corner there was a tree under which he read *Treasure Island*. It remained a favourite story for the rest of his life. But the world of the compound and the child that in memory he could see 'leaning over the warm handrail of the high veranda' was severed from him for ever. It seemed almost not to be a part of him, like 'some half-forgotten story in a book'.

He was sent to the grammar school in the British Concession, riding there each morning on a donkey. Most holidays were spent on the coast at Chefoo (*Yantai*), where his elder brother, my uncle Lonnie, was at boarding-school. Only in the summer of 1919 did the family return to Kuling.

A Letter from China   By Mervyn Peake

OUR station is Tientsin. My father has a hospital there. It is now fifty years old ; all the Chinese like it best. In the hospital we have three little Chinese boys, all lame. Two were run over on the railway, and one had a disease of the knee, so he had to have the leg cut off. We have adopted them because none of them know where their fathers and mothers are, and don't want to leave us. One of them helps the Chinese woman who mends the hospital clothes, by turning the handle of the sewing machine for her, but he would much rather play with the other boys. My father does not know what to do with these three boys. One of them, who will never be able to walk properly, may be taught the trade of a tailor, and perhaps the other two might be taught some other trade. My father and mother and I are coming to England. Our ship is going to start on the 15th of December.

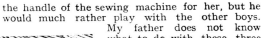

Mervyn's sketch

Above

Dr Peake outside the MacKenzie Memorial Hospital in Tientsin

Left

Mervyn Peake's first publication, in *News from Afar*, November 1922

IMAGE COURTESY OF UNIVERSITY COLLEGE LONDON

Ways of Travelling

Written and Illustrated by Mervyn L. Peake, of North China, aged 10½ years.

THERE are many ways of travelling in the world, such as by aeroplane, which travels at a great speed over the earth, and by submarine under the water. These were much used in the Great War.

In Africa the bullock wag-gon is used by the natives. It has a cover something like a Peking cart.

The camel is a very good journey maker, because it can carry very heavy loads, and also can go without food or drink for many days. One day when I was in a motor-car in Peking, when I was seven years old, I counted about one hundred camels.

I am now going to describe some ways by which I have travelled myself.

The first travelling I ever did was in a mountain-chair, from Kuling, when I was only five months old. I was carried shoulder high by four very sure-footed Chinese, while one false step on un-even ground would carry all five of us hundreds of feet below. From the chair I went on to a Yangtze river steamer. The steamer was very nice and comfortable. I know, because I have been on some since. They are much smaller than any ordinary sea steamer.

From Changsha I went into a " native house-boat " or junk for several hundreds of miles to Hengchow. The Chinese junk can travel in four different ways. Firstly, the boatmen can pull up the sails so that the wind catches them and then the boat goes very fast. Secondly, the boatmen go on to the shore and pull the junk along by ropes. That is called tracking. They also can take long poles and walk up and down the deck pushing them into the mud, shouting " Hey-ho."

This is called poling. The fourth way is to paddle or row with long oars to get along when the water is very deep. When the wind is blowing hard against, then they have to tie up to the shore until the wind is over. Once the boat that I was on was stuck in the Tung-Ting lake and for ten days we could not get away because of the wind.

The rickshas are about the commonest ways of travelling in the ports of China. They are like a chair with wheels, drawn by a man between two shafts. They are very convenient to go to any place, not very far away, for a few coppers.

I used to go to school on a donkey, and it was great fun, because he used to gallop like anything, but now I go to school on a bicycle. It is very useful for getting about on nice smooth roads, but one must look out for punctures.

I once rode in a Peking cart in Tsang-Chow. There is a mule between two shafts pulling a covered over cart. The cart has no springs, so that it bumps terribly, so that it makes your bones very sore.

The driver sits on the shafts very near the mule's tail. The people inside are usually very cramped.

I have been on many train journeys, but my longest was from China across Siberia to England. It took us just twelve days from Tientsin to London. We passed through Russia and we had Russian tea. Many of the Russian women sold us eatables like bread, milk and eggs.

My longest sea trip was from England to China in a Japanese steamer around the Cape. The whole journey took two months, and it was pretty risky because at that time the war was on and the German sub-marines were out.

Motor-cars are not at all rare in the streets of China now.

But the usual mode of travel-ling is on your feet, and it is generally the most convenient and the best.

Top left
Mervyn Peake photographed at about twelve months with the infant son of a Chinese doctor who worked under Dr Peake

Top right
Mervyn Peake's second publication, in *News from Afar*, January 1924

Above
Chinaman with a bird; a pencil drawing from the manuscript of *Titus IV* (late 1950s)

In his notes for an autobiography my father makes no mention of drawing, but I know that he started at an early age and never stopped. My grandparents recog-nized his talents and supported his early attempts to record what he saw around him. They allowed him to paint and draw at the living-room table, and he used to complain at having to clear away his paper, pencil and paints for mealtimes.

Another English boy that my father played with, climbing trees and along the compound wall, was Andrew Murray, who later became a well-known painter of greeting cards. In 1980, he recalled that 'Mervyn was always very kind and friendly to me, although I was five years younger. One day he found me drawing a ship sailing through sea. I had drawn the waves with curved, rounded tops; he suggested that they would look better with pointed crests. Ever since, I have put pointed tops to waves when I draw them.'

My father often told me that Mandarin was his first language, for my grandparents had found a calligraphy expert to teach him the formation of Mandarin characters. When I misbehaved he would sometimes reprimand me with an expression remembered from his youth. On the rare occasion when I actually was good we would count from one to a hundred together in Mandarin, an ability I still retain.

Doc found the north 'very different from the central and southern regions. We had left behind us the China of the picture books and had reached instead a dry and weary land.' Fine sand blown from the Gobi desert would darken the sky 'as by a great pall of yellow fog. It penetrates your clothes, your hair, your eyes, ears and nose, and grits between your teeth. It was an experience we never had to contend with in the damp, green regions of the south.'

Tientsin itself is situated some seventy miles to the south-east of Peking (*Beijing*), a city that fascinated Doc. 'It forms a perfect square, enclosed within massive battlemented walls and colossal gateways. Within it, like a square within a square, is the Imperial City, itself surrounded by high walls over six miles in circumference.' Shortly after the enforced abdication of the Boy-Emperor, Doc had 'special opportunity of entrance into the Forbidden City and viewed the beautiful palaces, lotus lakes, and temples. But an air of sadness and desolation pervaded the whole place. No life stirred within the deserted precincts.'

The ritual-bound life of the Emperors in a citadel cut off from the world may well have been a source of inspiration for Gormenghast. Each emperor seems to have added a temple or a courtyard, just as each earl contributed his building, until the castle became as large, as old, and as empty as the Eternal City. Be that as it may, the other sight that greatly impressed Doc certainly found its way into *Titus Groan*. The Chinese used to build avenues lined with massive sculptures of real and mythical creatures, along which the spirit of a dead emperor would journey to its resting place. Doc came across one such Spirit Way that he photographed. In the Hall of

Above left
Bactrian camel train outside the walls of Peking, photographed by Dr Peake

Above right
Mervyn Peake on his mother's knee, with his brother Leslie, Poole, 1915, on leave from China

Bright Carvings at Gormenghast the sculptures are seen 'in narrowing perspective like the highway for an Emperor'.

My father never forgot his time in China. It remained a primary influence, a constant backdrop to much of his writing and painting, poetry and illustration. Of northern China he remembered the great trains of roped-together shaggy, bactrian camels, donkeys and mules, the silk-clad mandarins, the ubiquitous pigtail, temples and pagodas, sedan chairs and sweating coolies, blue-tiled roofscapes, ceramic dragons and, above all, the eternal rituals that still dominated Chinese life. All these left an indelible impression.

Top left
Patient being carried to hospital

Above left
The Marble Boat at the Summer Palace, Peking, photographed by Dr Peake

Above right
Dr Peake (in white) and his staff outside the MacKenzie Memorial Hospital, Tientsin

Right
The view from inside the Marble Boat (with Dr Logan, a colleague), photographed by Dr Peake

Left
The Spirit Way to the Eastern
Imperial Tombs, photographed
by Dr Peake

Above
Family group, Tientsin, c.1919

2 The Evolving Artist

G. PETER WINNINGTON

One is clumsy at first. So is the apprentice of any skilled craft . . . The secret is to draw with intelligence – to be sure of what you want; for if you are undecided, so will your drawing be.

Mervyn Peake

Facing page
Self-portrait in oils submitted to the Royal Academy, 1931

Above
Mervyn Peake at Eltham College, *c.*1924

The Peakes returned to England early in 1923 and sent Mervyn to boarding-school at Eltham, south-east London. Endowed as a 'School for the Sons of Missionaries', Eltham was recovering from a lack of good staffing during the First World War. Two Old Boys, Eric and H.B. Drake, began teaching there just before Mervyn arrived. With infectious enthusiasm they introduced modern educational methods, instituting individual projects, performances of plays and a wide range of reading. Their impact on Peake was lifelong, as was their respect for him. In 1946 he was a witness to Eric Drake's second marriage, and in 1949 H.B. accepted to stand godfather to Peake's daughter Clare. In the 1980s Eric (by then long retired from teaching in Australia) was still enthusing about his old pupil's prose, poetry and illustrations.

At school Peake excelled at sports rather than in the classroom. He played in the school rugby team and did well in athletics, for he grew tall and lithe. 'My first memory of Mervyn', wrote Andrew Murray, who went to Eltham in 1927, 'is of him playing wing three-quarter for the first XV, tearing down the touchline at great speed, his dark, lank locks hanging over his eyes. He played with great abandon.' He was popular with the other boys, cultivating a 'pirate Peake' personality and drawing many pictures of pirates. For Eric Drake, the sketches which filled the margins of his school notebooks were 'quite brilliant in both perception and vitality'. In fact, it was Peake's drawing that saved him when the school considered sending him down for lack of academic achievement. 'You may be turning out one of our greatest future Old Boys,' warned his art master, 'Mackie' McIver, and the headmaster relented.

After *Treasure Island* Peake's favourite adventure story was *Under the Serpent's Fang*, another tale of treasure-seeking. It was illustrated by Stanley L. Wood whose work he greatly admired. Wood was indeed one of the best illustrators of boys' stories in the early years of the twentieth century. Until the mid-1930s Peake generally signed his drawings 'Mervyn L. Peake' in homage to his god. Of his

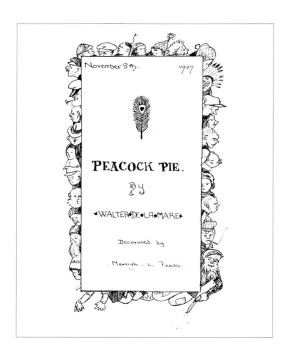

schoolboy writing only 'The White Chief of the Umzimbooboo Kaffirs' (printed in *Peake's Progress*) seems to have survived; his drawings can still be discovered in the autograph albums of his contemporaries.

On the other hand, Peake carefully preserved a twenty-seven-page series of illustrations that he made in the autumn of 1927 for poems by Walter de la Mare. At times, the style is not unreminiscent of E.H. Shepherd, whose work had regularly appeared in *Punch* since the early 1920s and whose illustrations for the Winnie the Pooh books came out during the three previous years. Whatever the influence, the penmanship is remarkably confident and assured for a sixteen-year-old.

Facing page, above and overleaf
Illustrations to Walter de la Mare's
Peacock Pie (1913), executed in
November 1927

SUMMER EVENING.

The sandy cat by the Farmers chair
Mews at his knee for dainty fare;
Old Rover in his moss-greened house
Mumbles a bone & barks at a mouse
In the dewy fields the cattle lie
Chewing the cud 'neath a fading sky
Dobbin at manger pulls his hay:
Gone is another summers day.

ANDY BATTLE

Once there was a young sailor, yeo ho!
And he sailed out over the say
For the isles where pink coral and palm branches blow
And the fire-flies turn night into day.   Yeo ho!
And the fire-flies turn night into day.

But the DOLPHIN went down in a tempest, yeoho
And with three forsook sailors ashore,
The PORTINGALES took him where sugar canes grow,
Their slave for to be evermore,   Ye ho
Their slave for to be evermore.

With his musket for mother & brother, yeo ho
He warred with the Cannibals drear
In forests where panthers pad soft to and fro,
And the PONGO shakes noonday with fear, yeo ho
And the PONGO shakes noonday with fear.

Now lean with long travail, all wasted with woe
With a monkey for messmate & friend,
He sits 'neath the CROSS in the cankering snow,
And waits for his sorrowful end,   yeo ho
And waits for his sorrowful end.

THE BEES' SONG

Thousandz of thornz there be
On the Rozez where gozez
The Zebra of Zee:
Sleek, striped and hairy,
The steed of the fairy
Princess of Zee.

Heavy with blozzomz be
The Rozez that growzez
In the muckets of Zee,
Where grazez the Zebra,
Marked Abracadeebra
Of the princess of Zee

And he rozez the poziez
Of the Rozez that growzez
So luvez'm and freez,
With an eye dark and wary,
In search of a Fairy,
Whose rozez he knowzez
Were not honey'ed for he,
But to breath a sweet incense
To solace a Princess
Of far-away Zee.

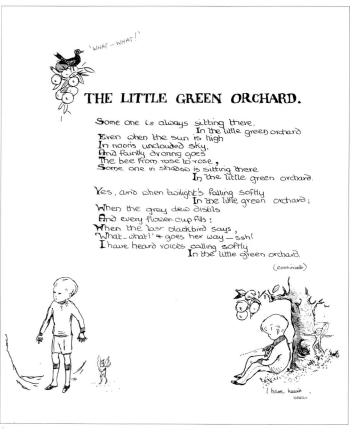

THE LITTLE GREEN ORCHARD.

Some one is always sitting there,
    In the little green orchard
Even when the sun is high
In noon's unclouded sky,
And faintly droning goes
The bee from rose to rose,
Some one in shadow is sitting there
    In the little green orchard.

Yes, and when twilight's falling softly
    In the little green orchard;
When the grey dew distils
And every flower-cup fills;
When the last blackbird says,
"What-what!" & goes her way—ssh!
I have heard voices calling softly
    In the little green orchard.

(continued)

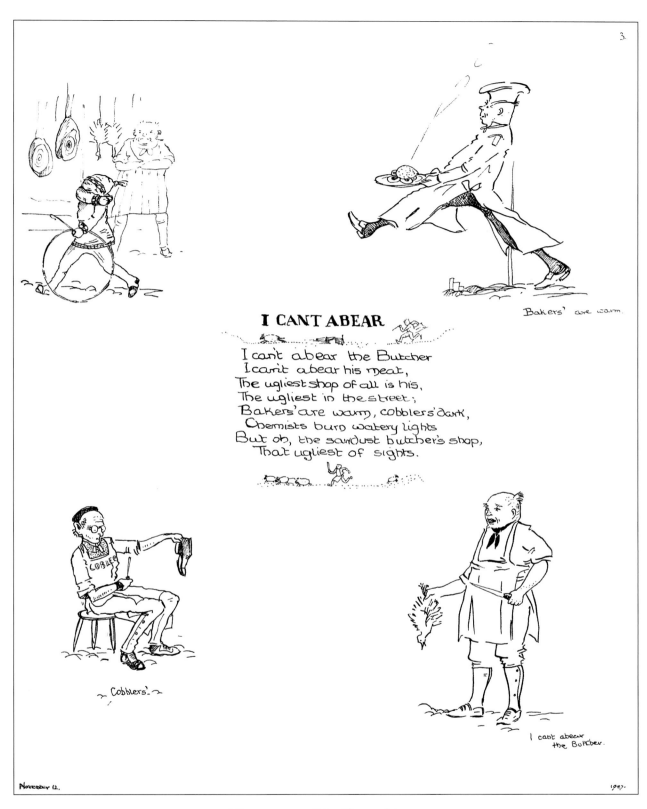

3.

Bakers' are warm.

I CANT ABEAR

I can't abear the Butcher
I can't abear his meat,
The ugliest shop of all is his,
The ugliest in the street;
Bakers' are warm, cobblers' dark,
Chemists burn watery lights
But oh, the sawdust butcher's shop,
That ugliest of sights.

Cobblers'.

I cant abear
the Butcher.

November 12.   1927.

On leaving Eltham, Peake attended the Croydon School of Art for a few months awaiting his admission to the Royal Academy Schools, which came in December 1929. That year he wrote his narrative poem, 'The Touch o' the Ash' (printed in *Peake's Progress*).

Up in London he developed a lifelong friendship with Gordon Smith, who was four years older and had just finished his studies at University College. Although Peake sat next to Gordon's brother in class at Eltham, it was only after leaving school that he and Gordon discovered their affinity for each other. Gordon – or 'Goatie', as Peake always called him – was something of a poet and would invent nonsensical rhymes about imaginary animals that Peake used to draw. The drawings inspired Goatie to further composition which in turn evoked more drawings. Collectively, the fantastic animals were Moccuses and at one point Peake made fair copies of their work in *The Moccus Book*, which they attempted to place with Chapman and Hall as a publication for children. It was turned down, but Peake never quite lost hope in the project. Some of the animals took on new life as inhabitants of the Yellow Creature's pink island in *Captain Slaughterboard Drops Anchor*.

In the summer of 1930 the two friends took a holiday together in France. Their first stopping point was Paris. Gordon Smith recalled how they

walked up the Champs Elysées discussing, rather childishly, the selection of an ideal World First Fifteen of painters. After considerable argument we agreed on a list of fourteen that included Rembrandt, Velasquez, Piero della Francesca and Botticelli. Leonardo, I think, was hooker. But we quarrelled about the last member of the side.

'For the last man,' said Mervyn firmly, 'we must have a stylist. I vote for Le Nain. He can play wing three-quarter.'

'Le Nain!' I exclaimed in horror. 'Goats and monkeys! Don't be daft; he wouldn't even make the Extra C.'

But Mervyn shook his head obstinately, and we went back down to the Louvre to check.

From Paris they moved on to the Puy de Dôme 'which turned out to be a most charming hummock, like a miniature Fujiyama'. Peake painted numerous watercolours on this expedition.

Top
Pencil portrait of Gordon Smith, *c.*1931

Right
Pirates from *The Three Principalities*, an unpublished book, *c.*1929; pen and ink

Facing page and overleaf
Characters from *The Moccus Book*, 1930

opposite page 19

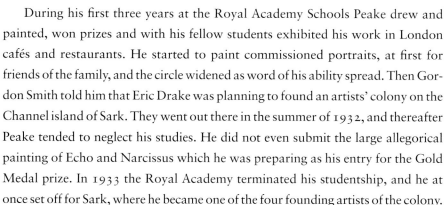

During his first three years at the Royal Academy Schools Peake drew and painted, won prizes and with his fellow students exhibited his work in London cafés and restaurants. He started to paint commissioned portraits, at first for friends of the family, and the circle widened as word of his ability spread. Then Gordon Smith told him that Eric Drake was planning to found an artists' colony on the Channel island of Sark. They went out there in the summer of 1932, and thereafter Peake tended to neglect his studies. He did not even submit the large allegorical painting of Echo and Narcissus which he was preparing as his entry for the Gold Medal prize. In 1933 the Royal Academy terminated his studentship, and he at once set off for Sark, where he became one of the four founding artists of the colony.

For some two years Peake painted Sarkese landscapes and seascapes and portraits of the local people (including some on Guernsey). He went to Chapman's circus when it paid its annual visit to the Channel Islands and produced drawings and paintings of clowns and circus animals, both of which remained favourite subjects for the rest of his life. His work was displayed in Eric Drake's gallery, which attracted tourists and professional exhibitors not only from Europe but also from Canada and the United States.

Reviewing Peake's animal studies, the *Guernsey Star* reported on 22 May 1934:

> The simplicity of line and the extraordinary effect of movement which he has imparted to these lightning impressions won the unstinted praise of every artist present . . . Polar bears balancing balls on their noses when Mervyn Peake draws them take on just that bearish note which makes one long to pat them every time they appear at a circus. Whether it is a dog or an elephant, the artist has the right intuition regarding each one, so much so that someone aptly remarked yesterday that you could almost smell them!

The colony survived for several years before internal tensions and financial difficulties got the better of it. Exactly when Peake left is not known, but on the strength of work shown in the Sark gallery he was offered a job as an assistant art master at the Westminster Art School in London. He started in February 1936 and proved to be an excellent teacher of life drawing.

He got on well with his students. 'His way of teaching was by drawing instructive sketches in the top left-hand corner of each student's paper,' recalls one of his earliest students, Diana Gardner. 'During the break, students would walk round to look at these drawings . . . Straight away, one was impressed by this method of teaching, of revealing through these sensitive drawings the way to observe the subject, by his patience and kindness – and by his shyness despite his intense good looks . . . The aim of his teaching was to illuminate, not to dominate.'

John Vernon Lord had a similar impression of Peake at the end of his teaching career, even though by then he

> was in a very bad way and seemed to be abstracted when he talked to you. Despite this illness, Peake had quite an effect on me during the three or four brief occasions we met. He made me think more deeply about the subject of illustration. I can recall him saying to me once, 'It is not only how you draw but what you draw, what you choose to put in the picture and what you decide to leave out.' Although I had very little contact with him, he was the first teacher to emphasise the power of content and atmosphere in pictures and how we should aim to create a mood in our illustrations that made the content live. At his best, Peake was one of the great illustrators, and I feel privileged to have had a glimpse of his teaching.

When Andrew Murray left school, he went to see Peake in his studio. After showing him round

> he took me to the Tate Gallery, which I had never visited before, enthusing about the Impressionists, Post-Impressionists and Cubists and scorning anything earlier. This was my first introduction to 'modern art' and was a formative event in the development of my taste. He also bought me some postcard prints of the painters he admired and started me off on collecting them.

Being back in London made it easier for Peake to place his work in periodicals. He became an occasional contributor of poems to the *London Mercury*, for instance, and 'attracted a good deal of notice in both the art and literary worlds by his pencil portraits of famous writers and poets, which revealed him as a great new master of line'.

Facing page
Characters from *The Moccus Book*
in pen and ink

Above
Animals from *The Moccus Book*;
pencil, pen and ink and watercolour

IMAGE COURTESY OF CHRIS BEETLES GALLERY

IMAGE COURTESY OF CHRIS BEETLES GALLERY

Above and left
Watercolour sketches produced
during a visit to the Puy-de-Dôme
with Gordon Smith, summer 1930

Facing page
Stunted trees on Sark; mixed
media, 1930s

This page
Sarkese fishermen on Sark, in oils, pencil, and pen and ink respectively, 1933–5

Facing page
The actress Flora Robson, later Dame Flora, drawn in pencil for the *London Mercury*, 1937

Overleaf, left
The actress Peggy Ashcroft, a pencil portrait commissioned by but not published in the *London Mercury*, 1937

Overleaf, right
The actress Monica Macdonald, whose family lived close by the Peakes; an oil painting from 1932

3 Husband and Father

G. PETER WINNINGTON

For Maeve

You are the maeve of me as this my arm
Is the joined arm of me; the heart within
Which I have heard so long yet never seen
Is thus – like these, you are my fount, my limb –
Yet more than these: you are the maeve of me.

Birthbed or deathbed, cradle and grave of me.
What is there that I lack? Yet what have I
More palpable than the immuring sky?
I can be lost in a familiar realm,
The more my knowledge the more lost to be
In all you are who are the maeve of me.

Mervyn Peake

On the first day of Peake's first full academic year at the Westminster, in September 1936, he noticed a new girl in the sculpture class and invited her to take a walk with him in the park.

'Out of my appalling shyness', she recalled years later, 'I said that I never went for walks and I didn't like parks. Perhaps such a bald answer should have ended everything before it began, but I did manage to ask, "What do you paint?" and the answer, "I'd paint a dustbin if I thought it beautiful", was by far the strangest thing I had ever heard, especially coming from the most romantic-looking man I had ever seen, that I managed to accept an invitation to tea, which followed this startling dustbin manifesto.'

Diana Gardner tells how, a year later, Peake mentioned to his students,

almost in passing, that he was going to be married . . . The woman chosen was also at the Westminster but not known to anyone in the Life class because she worked quietly downstairs in Eric Schilsky's sculpture class . . . A collection of students went down in the break to become acquainted . . . Maeve Gilmore, in a linen smock, Roman sandals, and with her light gold hair scraped back into a knot and pinned, and with two-inch heavy gold earrings hanging from small earlobes, could be recognized instantly as an artist's archetypal human being, straight out of a Florentine painting.

Facing page
Maeve drying her hair

In one of Peake's poems, 'To Maeve', he told her:

You walk unaware
Of the slender gazelle
That moves as you move
And is one with the limbs
That you have.

You live unaware
Of the faint, the unearthly
Echo of hooves
That within your white streams
Of clear clay that I love

Are in flight as you turn,
As you stand, as you move,
As you sleep, for the slender
Gazelle never rests
In your ivory grove.

Above
Two pencil studies of Maeve

Facing page
Self-portrait with beard, drawn
in pencil, Sark, 1938

Mervyn Peake and Maeve Gilmore married in December 1937. For their honeymoon they went by train down to Burpham, Sussex, where Doc had built himself a house for his retirement. The following year they had a second honeymoon on Sark. There Peake let his beard grow, just for once, and drew a self-portrait, looking somewhat bemused at his unfamiliar appearance. Maeve, however, was his most frequent subject; early in 1939 he estimated that he had already depicted her more than 750 times. Even his pirate story, *Captain Slaughterboard Drops Anchor*, published in October 1939, can be read as a fantasy version of their romance.

The Westminster Art School closed when the war broke out, and at the end of the year Mervyn and Maeve moved to a cottage close to Doc's. This was but the first of many removals. They rented various cottages around Burpham and then, towards the end of the war, returned to London, where they lived in studios. In 1946 they took a house on Sark, but by 1950 they were back in London again and Peake returned to teaching, at the Central School this time. They bought a house they really could not afford in Smarden, Kent, took over the family house in Wallington, Surrey, and finally settled in Chelsea. For their children it seemed a nomadic existence.

Their first child, Sebastian, was born in January 1940. The occasion inspired Peake with a poem, beginning:

Grottoed beneath your ribs our babe lay thriving
On the wild saps of Eden's midnight garden,
When qualms of love set fire the nine-month burden,
And there were phantoms in the cumulous sky,
And one green meteor with a flickering
Trail that stayed always yet was always moving;
O alchemy!
The fire-boy knocking at the osseous belfry
Where thuds the double-throated chord of loving.

Grottoed beneath your ribs, our babe no more
May hear the tolling of your sultry gong
Above him where the echoes throb and throng
Among the breathing rafters of sweet bone;
No longer coiled in gloom, the tireless core
And fount of his faint heart-beat fled,
He lies alone
With air and time about him and the drone
Of space for his immeasurable bed.

As Peake was at home, awaiting his call-up papers, he had time to make numerous drawings of his son. A portrait of Maeve with Sebastian became the frontispiece for the collection of nursery rhymes, *Ride a Cock-Horse*, that he illustrated for Chatto and Windus, published at the end of 1940.

Their second son, Fabian, was born in April 1942 while Peake was stationed up in Lancashire. He went AWOL to go to see him and Maeve, so it was of necessity a flying visit. In 1949 they had a daughter, Clare, on which occasion they were all together under one roof, on Sark.

Top
Maeve and Mervyn drawing each other; a press photograph on the occasion of their simultaneous but separate exhibitions, February 1939

Far right
Mervyn Peake in army uniform, early 1940s

Right
Pencil portrait of Peake's mother, mid-1930s

Facing page
Pencil sketches of Sebastian in 1940

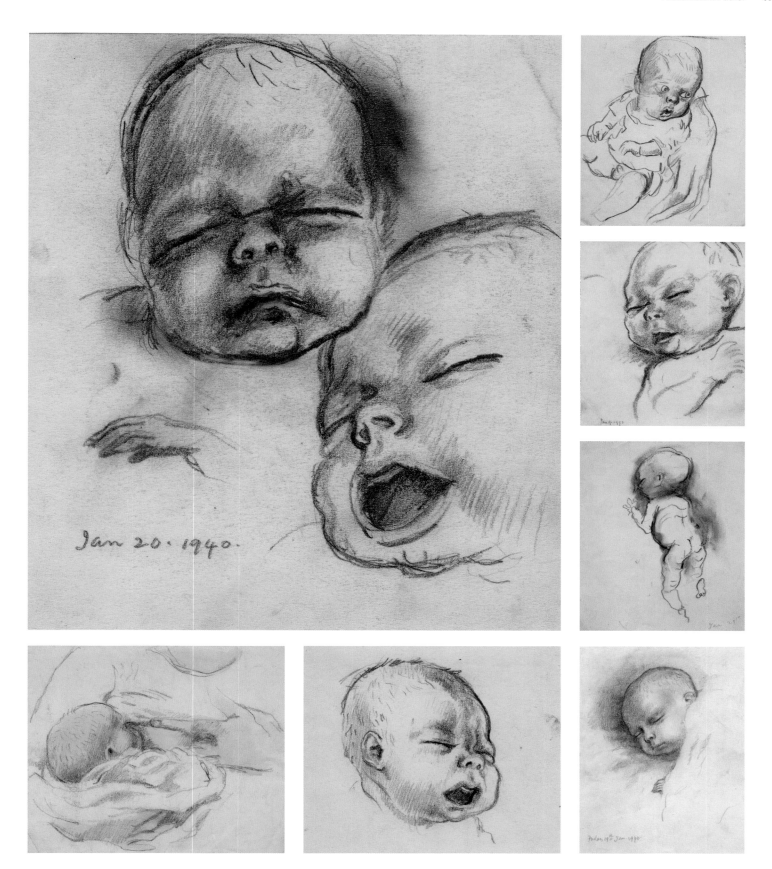

Jan 20. 1940.

Family photographs from the 1940s taken on Sark (with their donkey Judy), on Guernsey and in Sussex, including Dr Peake (above left) and (top right) Armand, who was the Peakes' gardener on Sark

Top left
Portrait of Fabian, late 1940s

Top right
Pirate Peake presents a cheque;
a sketch in pen and ink enclosed
with a cheque sent to his bank,
c. 1950

Centre right
A pencil portrait of Clare

Bottom
Two images from the Sunday
Books, in which Peake drew or
painted a picture each week for
his two sons, Sark, 1948; pen and
ink with watercolour

Doctor Foster went to Glo'ster

Doctor Foster went to Glo'ster
In a shower of rain ;
He stepped in a puddle,
Up to the middle,
And never went there again.

Jack Sprat

Jack Sprat could eat no fat,
His wife could eat no lean;
And so betwixt the two of them
They licked the platter clean.

Jack ate all the lean,
Joan ate all the fat,
The bone they picked it clean,
And gave it to the cat.

Rub-a-Dub-Dub

Rub-a-dub-dub,
Three men in a tub,
And who do you think they be ?
The butcher ; the baker ;
The candle-stick maker ;
Turn 'em out knaves all three.

Ride a Cock-Horse

Ride a cock-horse to Banbury Cross
To see a fine lady on a white horse ;
Rings on her fingers and bells on her toes,
She shall have music wherever she goes.

Facing page and above
Four illustrated nursery rhymes
from *Ride a Cock-Horse*; pen and
ink, overlaid with stencilled colour

Illustrations for *Ride a Cock-Horse*
in pen and ink

Above
'Old King Cole'

Top right
'How many miles to Babylon?'

Bottom
Frontispiece, for which Maeve and
Sebastian served as models

Facing page
'I saw a Peacock'

Maeve

MICHAEL MOORCOCK

IMAGE COURTESY OF CHRIS BEETLES GALLERY

Above
A study in wash of Maeve, *c.* 1940

I was a teenager when Maeve Gilmore first invited me to tea one September Sunday, to the mock-Gothic house in Wallington full of books and paintings and stuffed birds, and I think she was amused by me. I was probably pretty naïve, and my references to the Sexton Blake Library and the various children's magazines I worked for at the time must have seemed very peculiar. But she invited me back and began a friendship between her family and me which has lasted nearly fifty years.

I attended most of her openings and saw her paintings become more and more substantial, increasingly complex and technically adventurous. I own several, including a coloured drawing – a kind of harlequin and harlequina, one of a series in which she represented her relationship with her husband, sometimes celebrating, sometimes mourning.

Maeve was a beautiful woman. She had honey-blonde hair and hazel eyes (wasp-coloured in the words of one of the many poems written for her), and her complexion was like ivory, warm in the gentle sun. The quiet dignity of her manner, the apparent serenity which reflected a shy self-respect, made her more romantic admirers, like Dylan Thomas, compare her to a goddess. But since she was so rarely able to disguise her feelings about people, her face, revealing her thoughts, even when she attempted to be non-committal, was always supremely human. She remained fundamentally shy but learned to present a confident face to a world which became increasingly demanding.

She was born into a large and rather strict Roman Catholic family, educated at a convent and then, as a concession to her talents, allowed to attend the Westminster School, studying sculpture. It was on her first day there that she met her husband, a young teacher already beginning to make a name for himself as a painter and whose eccentric wit and magical personality captured her imagination.

It is impossible to say now which of the two was the more talented or whether Maeve, rather than taking the role of wife, mother and, later, manager of her husband's affairs, would have become as famous as he has. Her own work, sometimes

delicate, sometimes raw, was of a different kind, interpretative where his best-known work was more aggressively impositional. She never regretted that role and she recalled marvellous, fulfilling, happy times in Kent, on Sark, in London and Surrey, with her husband and their three children. She felt her first twenty years or so of marriage were frequently idyllic, a life which even a world war could not seriously threaten.

When I met Maeve, the best years were almost over, although that became obvious only as her husband's disease worsened and surgery exacerbated his condition. We now know that he had a form of Parkinson's disease, but in the late 1950s there was much to be discovered about such things. Maeve still had about her the air of the unworldly young woman who had lived an almost fairytale life with her family, painting side by side with her husband, raising children who spent much of their early lives in a rural paradise. I don't think it too melodramatic to say that she went from heaven into hell in a relatively short space of time, and it was a tribute to her character that she adapted to the change with unusual courage.

Maeve did everything she could to keep her husband at home and help him to work. Her own work suffered, of course, and it was not until she at last admitted the impossibility of his remaining at home, even with a full-time nurse, that she eventually began work again. She had taken charge of all his financial and publishing affairs, she cared for her growing children in their sometimes baffled distress, she helped organize exhibitions of her husband's art and, finally, she began to produce her own paintings of extraordinary power.

Her work became darker, angrier and more intense. Agonized figures stared helplessly from useless bodies; female forms supported male forms frequently crucified or tortured; terrified lovers embraced. All of Maeve's thoughts and feelings emerged in those canvases which were so powerful, so directly a record of the

Works by Maeve Gilmore

Above left
An oil painting of significant objects in her life: vertebrae collected by Mervyn from a dead whale washed up on a Sark beach in the 1930s, a music score (she was an accomplished pianist) and echoes of Raphael in the figures at the window.

Above right
A pencil drawing of Christ-like figures. After Mervyn's death, in an attempt to make sense of his suffering, she frequently depicted him as a Christ figure. This accompanied her own loss of faith. It was as though she was repeating the words scrawled on a cell wall at Auschwitz: 'If there is a God, where are you now?'

Above

Battersea, 1936. When he started teaching at the Westminster, Mervyn Peake rented rooms close to the Thames. For their early meetings Maeve was driven there by the family chauffeur, who would wait outside.

horror of what was happening, that the galleries which had earlier taken an interest in her work now began to recoil, virtually demanding that she return to a more modest or delicate style, something perhaps in tune with their preferred image of her as the wounded handmaiden to Genius.

Maeve was always her own woman. For all the love and extraordinary kindness she exhibited (to my wife Linda, among many others) she was never given to sentimentality. She claimed to dislike babies, yet painted a wonderland of murals in the upstairs rooms of her house, just for the delight of her nine grandchildren. Indeed, the whole of her house in Drayton Gardens, Kensington, was alive with murals – in the kitchen, the hallways, on the stairs and on the screens she began to paint, originally as an idea for raising much-needed money and later for her own pleasure. There were also knitted dolls – Pierrot, Columbine and others – which eventually became the characters in her only children's book, *Captain Eustace and the Magic Room*. It reproduces Kenneth Welfare's photographs of the dolls against some of the murals, thus preserving them, for the house was sold after Maeve's death and the new owner destroyed them. Maeve's other book was an account of her life with

Mervyn Peake. It is called *A World Away* and in its directness, its recollection of happiness, it remains one of the most moving memoirs I have ever read.

After many years of distress and struggle, during which Mervyn died in 1968, life began to improve for her, while her arthritis worsened. In 1983, she went into hospital for a hip replacement and eventually she was told that she had bone cancer. Understanding that she did not have very long to live, she faced this last disaster with the same directness and courage she had faced the others, her concern for her family and close friends as considerable as always.

She was buried in the village churchyard at Burpham, Sussex, beside her husband. At her funeral the vicar praised her for being a wonderful wife and mother and eulogized her husband's gifts.

Mervyn would have been the first to want it made clear that her gifts were as outstanding as his own. Her generosity, her sensitivity, her practicality, her humour and her dignity were just a few of the qualities which, added to her marvellous talent, made her a person whom I still love and who remains vividly alive in my heart. I shall never cease to miss her. She will always be with me.

Above left
A line portrait of Maeve

Above right
Maeve at Burpham, 1950s

4 War Artist

G. PETER WINNINGTON

The Army would be glad to get rid of me, I think. Being unmechanical I do not fit into their scheme of things at all and they try and find fatuous jobs for me.

Gunner Peake, 228. D. T. Rgt, RA

Facing page
Hankow burning – during and after. Photographs by Dr Peake, taken in 1911

Above
The head of a summarily executed looter hung up as a warning to others; photograph by Dr Peake, Hankow, 1911

While Peake was producing exquisite illustrations for *Ride a Cock-Horse*, war was raging on the Continent. After Poland, Hitler attacked Scandinavia and then, in mid-1940, rapidly overran Holland, Belgium and most of France. Peake wanted to contribute his skill as an artist to the war effort, but the War Artists' Advisory Committee (WAAC) shelved his application. Undeterred, he imagined a propaganda leaflet in the form of a portfolio of pictures by the artist Hitler. The titles were conventional, such as 'Mother and Child' or 'Landscape with Figures', but they depicted a woman mourning her murdered infant or peasants being shot. Although the Ministry of Information was initially excited by the series, and proposed using the pamphlet in South America, nothing came of it in the end. Most of the twenty-five pictures went into the archives of the Public Record Office; the sequence has never been published in full.

It was not until much later that the atrocities committed during the war were shown to the public, but Peake's imagination was prescient. It had been fed by gory photographs in the family album, taken by his father in the Chinese revolution of 1911.

Another series of what we might call Peake's personal propaganda was exhibited in 1941 at the American British Art Center in New York, alongside photographs of 'London's Honorable Scars' by Cecil Beaton. As they do not appear to have been seen since, by anyone, we can only speculate that, with titles such as 'Love's Old Sweet Song', 'Sleeping Partner', 'Lebensraum' and 'Full-Length Portrait by Hitler', they were similar in inspiration to the first series.

Peake struggled hard to be given work as a war artist, writing letter after letter to Sir Kenneth Clark, who as director of the National Gallery was also chairman of the WAAC. Despite Clark's letters of recommendation, the Army persisted for two-and-a-half years in trying to fit this square peg into round holes, driving Peake almost to despair. 'Granted, I'm hopeless,' he told Gordon Smith, 'but I wouldn't be if they'd put me into something where my talent could be used.' Ultimately, abandoned in a transit camp up at Clitheroe, he had a nervous breakdown.

While on medical leave from the Army, he worked for six months in the propaganda department of the Ministry of Information. Exactly what he did there is not known, but a postcard lampooning Hitler and Mussolini as a wedding couple surfaced quite recently, and it probably dates from this period. Then, in January 1943, the WAAC finally got round to giving Peake an opportunity to contribute to the war effort. He was sent to the glass works of Chance Brothers in Smethwick to paint the manufacture of cathode-ray tubes. This was the only factory in the country capable of producing the screens on which early radar sets displayed their vital information. Peake made numerous sketches, drawings and then paintings of the men at work and wrote a poem about it. This became the title poem of a collection of his verse for which, in conjunction with *Gormenghast*, he was awarded the 1950 Heinemann Prize for literature.

"ATÉ QUE A MORTE NOS SEPARE"
Caricatura de Mervyn Peake

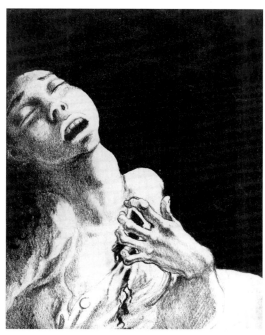

Facing page
'Self-portrait' from Peake's imaginary portfolio by the artist Hitler

Top left
Peasant Dance

Bottom left
Polish Dawn

Top right
Hitler and Mussolini as a wedding couple; a propaganda postcard drawn for the Ministry of Information

Centre right
Title page with palette

Bottom right
Study of a Young Girl; mixed media

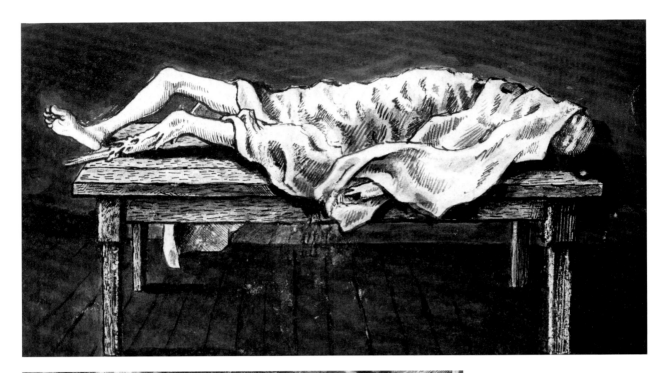

Further works from the portfolio
by Hitler

Top
Still Life

Centre
Landscape with Figures

Bottom
Dutch Interior; pen and ink with
watercolour washes

Top
Family Group, 1940

Above left
Young Girl

Above centre
Mother and Child

Above right
Reclining Figure; mixed media

Glass-blowers at work, showing stages in forming a cathode-ray tube; pen and ink

Top left
Gathering at the furnace

Centre left and right
Blowing

Bottom left
Holding up the finished tube

Bottom right
Examining the gobbet of glass

The Glass Blowers

MERVYN PEAKE

Darkness, brickwork; hall after mammoth hall, pseudo-archaic, absurd, begrimed, impressive, sinister; a setting for some film of gloomy passion. The grey spaces, ponderous gates, and ugly towers. Crumbling and obsolete in every corner. In this huge womb, fires roar. Furnaces like the mouths of tigers yell with their hundred tongues in every throat. Such a place shall never be built again. It is a theatre; an adumbrate setting for fire-lit figures that cast inordinate shadows. The gloom is full of gestures, suddenly lit, as suddenly swallowed. It is full of twists and turns of the body, of the head, of the schooled limbs. The heavy feet move by. The heads of workmen watch the molten growth. Between the head and feet a rhythm of clay, as in coarse hands, deft hands, the long pipe spins.

What is this fruit that burns like blood and fire, cools into gold, into green, flushes with indescribable blues, shivers into opal? What is happening?

It is the ballet of glass. It is the ballet of dark hours; of furnace-heat. It is the ballet of sweat. The ballet that not one of these deft craftsmen knows for such. Rough-clothed, rough-headed, drenched with sweat, they are yet as delicate as dancers.

One man comes forward. He gathers at the furnace mouth the roaring, white-hot sand – gathers it at the tip of the long pipe, twirls it as he gathers, twirls it as he withdraws the metal flute, juggles with it, spins it, and at the millionth moment puffs at the pipe-head, and the clinging spilth swells with his breath into a blinding gourd. Now this way, now that, giving it breath or swinging the long instrument so that the ductile sand, budding and semi-liquid, burgeons forth into a great whale of light, or a snake-shaped length, only to be puffed out again and twisted as it cools, swung and withdrawn, until at the tick of temperature, the pipe is rested over the water trough to speed the cooling. The swivelling never for a moment ceasing, until, given breath once more, the blood-red thing is lowered: lowered gradually,

Above
Preliminary sketch

spinning as it descends, over a little cliff of brick, where wait the moulds, their great iron mouths agape. Carefully, spinningly, the pendant gob descends, lighting the glassman's hand with its fury: descends into the mould. The jaws close and in the metal cage the fruit spins on, while bending over the cliff edge, his cheeks blown out like fruits of gold themselves, the glassman twirls and puffs, his head now at this angle and now at that, the strands of his throat taut as bow-strings, his body deft to every whim of the glass. Rhythmic in adjustment, he is the lyric-juggler, half fire-lit angle, half cheek-blown gargoyle.

He taps his foot upon the brick-edge cliff. The mould flies open and, taking the pipe from his mouth, he lifts and sweeps up from beneath an exact, symmetrical transparency still roseate from the furnace. Rapidly now it cools as he withdraws into the darkness of the factory, the glimmering object changing hue with every step he takes; now gold, now saffron, now apple-green, now jade, and all the thousand tints that lie between until, as he places it among its kind, knocking the glass head from the pipe with frightening ease, it is perfect, translucent, white with the cold that is about it and in it. That head once white with searing heat – that head that was once even earlier, perhaps, the sea-domed castle of some long-dead child.

Far from gull-wailing strands, it has become the burning mother of transparency. Sand. No longer the fast sky; the coughing wave. Girdled in a grey fastness of masonry, welkined with crasser substance than the clouds, it has found its purpose. And from its huge transmutation lucence breaks.

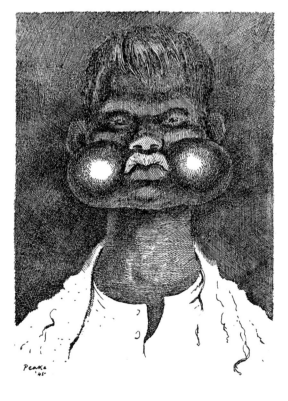

Top left
One of Peake's finished oil paintings of a glass-blower at work

Centre
Finished pen-and-ink portrait of glass-blower 'with cheeks blown out like fruits of gold'

Other pictures, here and on facing page
Preliminary sketches and paintings in various media for the glass-blowers commission

Girl dying of consumption at Belsen, a month after the Burning.

Belsen

In the end, Peake was given only two commissions as an official war artist. He found the second – drawing bomber crews before and after their missions over the Continent – far less inspiring.

In 1945, though, just as the war in Europe was ending, he managed to land a contract with a magazine, the *New Leader*, to accompany the young journalist Tom Pocock to the Continent. The idea was that Peake would provide illustrations to Pocock's articles. After Paris, where Peake drew pictures of the nightlife thronged with GIs, they flew into Germany. He was horrified to see the ruined towns, the haggard and hostile population, the massed prisoners of war and, worst of all, the remaining inmates of the camp at Bergen-Belsen. It was barely six weeks since the camp had been liberated, and the prisoners who remained were those who were too ill to be moved; they were literally dying before his eyes as he sketched them. He tried to verbalize his emotions in verse, but it was an experience from which Maeve felt that he never really recovered.

The Consumptive
Belsen, 1945

I
If seeing her an hour before her last
Weak cough into all blackness I could yet
Be held by chalk-white walls, and by the great
Ash coloured bed,
And the pillows hardly creased
By the tapping of her little cough-jerked head –
If such can be a painter's ecstasy,
(Her limbs like pipes, her head a china skull)
Then where is mercy?

The captions on this and the following page are Peake's own, taken from his book of *Drawings* (1949)

Facing page
Dying Girl in Blanket; charcoal

Above
Drawing of a Girl at Belsen, 1945; mixed media

And what

Is this my traffic? for my schooled eyes see

The ghost of a great painting, line and hue,

In this doomed girl of tallow?

O Jesus! has the world so white a yellow

As lifts her head by but a breath from linen

In the congested and yet empty world

Of plaster, cotton, and a little marl?

Than pallor what is there more terrible?

There lay the gall

Of that dead mouth of the world.

And at death's centre a torn garden trembled

In which her eyes like great hearts of black water

Shone in their wells of bone,

Brimmed to the well-heads of the coughing girl,

Pleading through history in that white garden;

And very wild, upon the small head's cheekbones,

As on high ridges in an icy dew,

Burned the sharp roses.

II

Her agony slides through me: am I glass

That grief can find no grip

Save for a moment when the quivering lip

And the coughing weaker than the broken wing

That, fluttering, shakes the life from a small bird

Caught me as in a nightmare? Nightmares pass;

The image blurs and the quick razor-edge

Of anger dulls, and pity dulls. O God,

That grief so glibly slides! The little badge

On either cheek was gathered from her blood:

Those coughs were her last words. They had no weight

Save that through them was made articulate

Earth's desolation on the alien bed.

Though I be glass, it shall not be betrayed,

That last weak cough of her small, trembling head.

Victims

They had no quiet and smoothèd sheets of death
To fold them and no pillows whiter than the wings
Of childhood's angels.
There was no hush of love. No silence flowered
About them, and no bland, enormous petals
Opened with stillness. Where was lavender
Or gentle light? Where were the coverlets
Of quiet? Or white hands to hold their bleeding
Claws that grabbed horribly for child or lover?
In twisting flames their twisting bodies blackened,
For History, that witless chronicler
Continued writing his long manuscript.

Mervyn Peake

Facing page
Girl of Seventeen Dying; charcoal

Below left
Girl Coughing; charcoal

Below right
Girl with Cropped Hair; charcoal

5 The Titus Books

I predict for Titus a smallish but fervent public which will probably renew itself, and probably enlarge, with each generation; for which reason I hope the book may always be kept in print.

Elizabeth Bowen

Facing page
Study of Fuchsia; pen and ink with watercolour wash, *c.* 1945

Below
Covers of the Penguin Modern Classics of 1968–70 and a sketch of Titus from the manuscript of *Gormenghast*

Peake was drafted into the Royal Artillery at the end of July 1940, just as he was starting on a story that was to grow under his pen into the three novels about Titus Groan. Given the circumstances, he wrote in notebooks that he could carry with him, rather than on loose sheets of paper that would easily go astray. Right from the start he made sketches as he went along, sometimes in the margins, sometimes on whole pages. Occasionally the text continues over a drawing. Some of these sketches depict the characters of the book; seeing them helped Peake to imagine what sort of things they would say. He rather hoped that *Titus Groan* might be illustrated with finished versions of these sketches, but the publisher turned down the idea. However, drawings from the manuscripts were used to decorate the second edition of the Titus books (and all the paperbacks that followed). Other pictures in the manuscripts range from finished pen drawings to abstract doodles. Some are quick portraits and sketches of scenes around him as he wrote, but most of them are from his imagination.

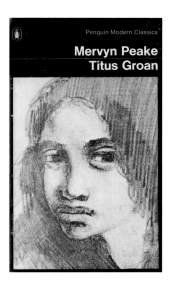

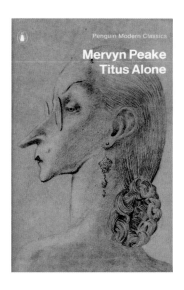

The Achievement of Mervyn Peake

MICHAEL MOORCOCK

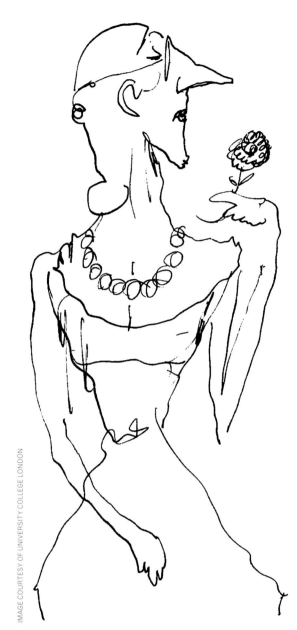

Fundamentally Peake's imagination was, without question, a romantic one, but, perhaps paradoxically, it is his humanity, his less idiosyncratic gifts (including the gift of farce), that distinguish him from other great visionary novelists such as Wyndham Lewis, Yevgeny Zamyatin or John Cowper Powys.

In the Titus Groan books especially, with their ornate language, long soliloquies, bursts of nonsense verse, vivid descriptions, weird anecdotes, comic extravagances, we continue to be interested in the characters and their stories. Peake's control of his subject matter, his skill at handling such a large cast, is demonstrated on every page of *Titus Groan* and *Gormenghast*, which are essentially a unity. The plot marches, with all the remorseless inevitability of a novel by Victor Hugo or Joseph Conrad, towards an unpredictable resolution.

These abilities and his genuine love of people, his concern for others, his relish for life, make Peake, in my opinion, the greatest imaginative writer of his age. Neither J. R. R. Tolkien nor T. H. White, for instance, has Peake's monumental complexity or originality, his moral and formal integrity. Perhaps that is why Peake was so often praised by writers most identified with naturalistic novels of character, such as Elizabeth Bowen or Angus Wilson, who also appreciated the moral qualities of Peake's novels. He offers a solid clue to his sentiments (and his method) in the opening sentence of *Titus Groan*:

> Gormenghast . . . would have displayed a certain ponderous architectural quality were it possible to have ignored . . . those mean dwellings that swarmed like an epidemic around its outer walls.

By the first few paragraphs of the first Titus novel our sympathies are already alerted. Peake is not merely writing Romance – he is examining Romance. He is, perhaps, even finding fault with it, or at least is looking for flaws in its arguments. He was of a generation that had seen the corrupt romanticism of Nazi Germany

infect most of Europe, and his conscience remained essentially that of a radical Christian. He admired Bunyan as well as Blake. He was attracted to the imagery of pomp and ritual, but he was also deeply suspicious of it, always searching for what it hid. In those early pages of *Titus Groan* we find blind injustice, decadent ritual and haughty cruelty, folly, moral corruption, atrophied emotions and sensibilities, wretched hypocrisy and dumb despair; turbulence and terror are masked by a pretence of activity, a reliance on ritual which in the end has no function save to maintain the status quo – the power of the Groans. Yet here, too, is all the dusty glory of a decadent court, ancient mysteries, bizarre secrets, peculiar dependencies and relationships, old rivalries, a history already so encrusted with legend and myth that it is no longer a record of events but a litany of blind faith.

This could be the China of Mervyn's boyhood translated to England. In that China the poor committed suicide on the surgery steps of doctors unable to cure them, and ancient wealth was displayed against a background of dreadful social suffering. It was an hallucinatory imperial twilight, common to all declining empires, which obscured the hardships of the many from the undemanding eyes of the privileged few – a light Mervyn detected in England, too. He was in many ways a conventional patriot, but he was also amused, frustrated and infuriated by the follies of the English ruling class. His own wartime experience of bureaucratic folly and the ignorant arrogance of leaders, the casual decisions which affected the lives and deaths of thousands, informed the pages of *Titus Groan* as he wrote it in various barracks, railway stations and transit camps while the army tried to make a gunner of him. Yet the novel never becomes a diatribe, never becomes a vehicle in which to express his own suffering.

By the time we finish *Titus Groan*, with all its wonders, its invention, its vast-ness, its confident eloquence, we have become engrossed in the fate of the boy,

Facing page
Sketch of Irma Prunesquallor in the manuscript of *Titus Groan*

Top left and centre
Sketches of Steerpike

Top right
Sketch of a Professor in the manuscript of *Gormenghast*

Above
Sketch of Maeve reading, from the manuscript of *Titus Groan*, pen and ink

Below left
Lithograph of Swelter made at the Central School of Art

Below right
The title page of one of the notebooks in which Peake wrote *Titus Groan*

Facing page

Upper left
Flay carrying Titus

Bottom left
A page opening from the manuscript of *Gormenghast* with sketches of professors

Bottom centre
The edge of Gormenghast forest

Bottom right
Fantastic seated figure

Titus, his relatives and retainers. By now we are intimately involved with Fuchsia Groan, Lord and Lady Groan, Nannie Slagg, Cora and Clarice, Rottcodd, Swelter, Flay, the Prunesquallors, the masters and all the others – but chiefly we want to know what has become of Steerpike.

Steerpike is Peake's greatest creation and, ultimately, in Gormenghast he confronts that fresh embodiment of the Groan tradition, the new Lord Titus, who has come into the title prematurely as a result of Steerpike's own machinations. Steerpike has something of the knowing, reckless villainy of Richard III, something of the cold, envying evil of Pinkie in *Brighton Rock*, and yet we frequently find ourselves feeling sympathy with his ambitions and his conflicts. We share his frustrations, his anger, his schemes, his secrets, his knowledge of all the illusions, hypocrisies and deceits required to maintain Groan power in that seemingly limit-less castle, that model of the mind, whose Gothic outlines bear only superficial resemblance to Walpole's or Radcliffe's.

Yet poor silly Cora and Clarice, dreamy Irma Prunesquallor and her ebullient, yet oddly pathetic brother also receive our concern because, even though they might seem grotesque or larger than life, their dreams, if not the details of their lives, are common to most of us. Their passions and desires, sadness and despair, are easily understood. There are no airy metaphysics in the Titus Groan books (unless for farcical effect), no comfy reassurances (unless from a hypocrite), no universal railing (unless from a fool). We follow Steerpike, who uses all the quick cunning and subtle understanding, all the knowing play-acting of a Lovelace, in his rise from kitchen boy to secret power of Gormenghast. His motives are credible. Again, from the first pages, Peake has led us to understand how an intelligent youth, destined for a life of humiliation and grinding servitude, is consumed with anger at the monumental injustices upon which his misfortune and the continuing fortunes of the Groans is based.

If Tolkien's hobbits display a middle-class fear of the Mob, Steerpike might be said to represent the vengeful Mob itself, all hope of justice lost, turning its ruthless fury upon those who, in their unearned, unadmitted power – no matter how innocent they seem to themselves – enjoy careless privilege. And, like the Mob, Steerpike is by no means fussy about his methods – and by no means invulnerable. Eventually common sentiment becomes both his doom and his redemption.

At the close of Gormenghast Titus begins to come into his own. Like Steerpike, he struggles against the weight of ritual and convention that imprisons him, but he struggles only to be free, not to control. He understands the price of such power and wants none of it.

In the final volume, *Titus Alone*, which was to be the first of a new set of adventures, Titus at last assumes centre stage. In the first two volumes he figures rather less than Tristram Shandy in the work named after him, but now he is a kind of wandering innocent, consciously based on Candide, adrift from his roots in Gormenghast, determined not to be crushed by the stifling decadence of his ancestors, yet knowing little of the world beyond the walls. With the help of the half-mad Muzzlehatch and Juno, who becomes Titus's lover, he makes a transition from the hermetic surreality of Gormenghast Castle to the bizarre realities of a world far more familiar to us.

Titus Alone is packed with images of authoritarianism, of the Blitz, of Belsen and all the other horrors which the Allies had witnessed as they moved through the nightmare the Nazis had made of Europe. Those who demanded from Peake a more specific moral examination than they found in the first two books found it here. For me, in many ways, *Titus Alone* is the best of the three novels, the most ambitious of them. It seemed to me that Mervyn was confronting and trying to reconcile his faith in human goodness with his personal experience of grotesque and brutal human evil.

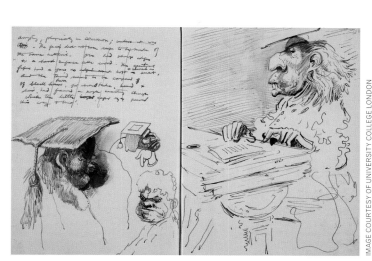

Discovering the Titus Books

JOANNE HARRIS

Above
Pen-and-ink sketch of a Professor
from the manuscript of
Gormenghast

Facing page

Top
A woman sketched in the Café
Royal, August 1941, from the
manuscript of *Titus Groan*

Bottom
Two boys with animals, from the
manuscript of *Mr Pye*

My thirteen-year-old daughter has just discovered another world. The symptoms first manifested themselves in a certain gleeful, gloating secretiveness; in homework neglected; and lately, in a string of unusual vocabulary queries. *Denizen. Octogenarian. Ponderous. Calid.*

I know these symptoms well, of course. I made a similar discovery at almost the same age, when, disenchanted with Narnia and sceptical of Wonderland, I found myself introduced, quite by accident, into a fictional world of such intensity and richness that, three decades later, I have still never really quite escaped, or really wanted to.

The world, of course, is Gormenghast. To an imaginative adolescent mind, it offers glories, glamours and a seemingly infinite sense of possibility. At fifteen I consumed the Titus books in a single week, then spent the next six weeks finding and devouring anything by or about Mervyn Peake I could lay my hands on – poetry; prose; plays; illustration; biography – before returning to the novels again and again with increasingly obsessive attention to the vocabulary, customs, characters and manifold idiosyncrasies of Gormenghast, the city-castle-microcosm that, even in absence (*Titus Alone*) forms the dense and inscrutable heart of the Titus books.

Since then, I have renewed my acquaintance with Gormenghast every few years and have found it changed at every visit. For Gormenghast, unlike Narnia, has no upper age limit to appreciation; Peake's finely crafted world is designed to age cleverly with the reader, continually providing new perspectives and areas for exploration.

As a fifteen-year-old I was captivated by the fulsomeness of Peake's creation; by the fabulous attention to detail; by the frequent conflicts between the individual and authority and the perpetual theme of revolt that resurfaces throughout the books. I loved the wondrous carnival of it; revelled in the grotesque; was intoxicated by the language; and copied it slavishly (and ludicrously) in my own writing.

By the age of twenty I had discovered both Kafka and Jung and was fascinated

IMAGE COURTESY OF UNIVERSITY COLLEGE LONDON

by the parallels. At thirty, and a mother, I had begun to appreciate the deep humour and deeper humanity of Peake's work and the effervescent sense of joy and wonder that underlies all his writing.

For Peake's writing is as mercurial as the man himself. For sixty years it has defied classification – and has therefore been sneeringly dismissed by some as 'fantasy writing' (as if real issues and real emotions could not possibly exist within such a context as an imaginary world). Its very virtuosity can be daunting; for Peake draws from an emotional and stylistic palette of such diversity that, to appreciate his work fully, the reader needs to jettison all preconceptions regarding genre, plot and structure and approach the books with a mind untrammelled by convention or bias.

The rewards of such an approach are manifold. Peake's world is built on a number of assumptions, one of which is the unquestioned acceptance of a status quo that is certainly eccentric and, in some cases, verging on the surreal. In a world seemingly out of time, where horses may swim in rooftop lakes and men are eaten

IMAGE COURTESY OF UNIVERSITY COLLEGE LONDON

Top row
Pen-and-ink sketches from the manuscript of *Gormenghast*:

Top left
Barquentine

Top centre and right
Fantastic figures

Above
Girl's head, titled *Furrie* by Peake, from the manuscript of *Titus Alone*, drawn with a felt-tipped pen

alive by wild owls, thoughts of what may or may not count as 'fantasy' seem both irrelevant and unnecessary.

And yet the Titus books are imbued with a profound sense of realism. Some of this comes from the hallucinatory attention that Peake gives to the smallest of details – shapes and textures; colours and scents; the jut of a collar-bone; the fuggy stench of subterranean kitchens; the cracking sound of a man's knee-joints as he strides stiffly along a stone corridor.

Interestingly, for a writer frequently described in terms of 'Gothic' and 'fantasy', there is no trace of the supernatural in the Titus books. There are no witches, no ghosts, no magic, no religion – but for the wholly secular ritual of Gormenghast. Nor is there any sign of the usual non-human suspects that tend to permeate fantasy fiction. To Peake, humanity itself already contains so much potential for grotesquerie that there is no need for orcs or dwarves. Instead we are shown a vision of humanity at its most diverse and perplexing. Physical and mental deformity abounds; and yet beneath Peake's obvious delight in portraying the human being in all its astonishing variety he retains a quality of insight and sympathy for his creations that raises his work beyond technical brilliance into something warmer and more universal.

Not that his technique is lacking at all. The phonetic impact of the language alone is stunning. Much has been written of Peake the literary draughtsman; but he also uses language much in the manner of Rimbaud or Baudelaire, with less thought to the accepted meaning of the word than to its rhythmic potential as a part of the sentence. This gives his narrative a thundering, biblical quality that is often more akin to poetry than prose – in his radio broadcast of June 1947 Peake mentions shifting from prose rhythms to poetic rhythms at moments of dramatic intensity, with the effect of heightening emotional tension. Like Rimbaud, Blake and Nabokov, he also speaks of the link between colour and sound, describing his characters' voices in shades of dark green or pale blue against the normal grey setting out

the dialogue as an artist constructs his palette. It is this hint of synaesthesia that, for me, gives the work its intrinsic 'total-immersion' effect, engaging all the senses to create something that is less of a narrative than a whole-body experience.

Although I have long since given up the attempt to copy Peake's flamboyant style in my writing, I'm aware that I still owe him a considerable artistic debt. In finding my own style I have tried over the years to assimilate some of the ideas that have struck me most forcibly from my reading of the Titus books. One is the importance of place and its role – which may be as important as that of any character or more so – within the body of the story. Another is the sensual quality of words and the way in which they can be used to evoke physical responses. Another is the importance of sound and rhythm on the written page (I always read my work aloud as I write, as Peake did).

I am far from alone in admitting such a debt; although Peake may still be considered by some as a relatively minor figure among the giants of the twentieth century, he casts a surprisingly long shadow. Neil Gaiman, Susannah Clarke, Michael Moorcock, China Miéville, Iain Banks, Philip Pullman, Robert Silverberg – all admit to having been influenced by him to some extent.

But perhaps the most important part of Peake's legacy to the would-be writer is his fierce individuality and his willingness to experiment with, to bend – and often even to break – the rules. In a world where literature seems to be getting progressively duller, smaller, safer and more homogenized, and where marketability, rather than originality, now determines what should and should not be published, Peake remains an inspiration to anyone who still feels, as I do, that the role of the writer is to challenge, rather than to conform; to question, rather than to answer, and to seek out the sublime over the saleable, the marvellous over the mundane. It is this quality that has kept Peake's work alive and fresh for sixty years. Long may it continue to inspire us, and may many more generations discover, as my daughter has, the charm of this most unruly and rebellious of literary figures.

Above left
Sleeping figure from the manuscript of *Gormenghast*

Above right
Titus in a prison cell: 'holding an iron bar with either hand, he stared across a landscape' (*Titus Alone*, p. 68); a sketch from the manuscript

6 The Craft of the Lead Pencil

While Peake was living on Sark, between 1946 and late 1949, he wrote *Gormenghast*, *The Rhyme of the Flying Bomb* and other poems, and drew many of his celebrated illustrations, including *Treasure Island*. Although he was not teaching during this period, he also wrote a little guide for art students, *The Craft of the Lead Pencil*, which sums up his approach to drawing and gives advice that many students have found invaluable. In the following section, Chris Riddell comments on it.

Facing page
Figure astride a friendly monster, from a visitors' book, 1939

Left
A girl's head lit from below, demonstrating how 'light and shade can force so strange a contrast'

Peake on Draughtsmanship

CHRIS RIDDELL

'To make a drawing is to record an idea: an idea of a particular breed that can only be expressed through making marks on a piece of paper.' Thus Mervyn Peake begins his discourse on the craft, not art, as he carefully tells us, of drawing. In this age of computer and video art, the simple contemplation of producing a drawing with a lead pencil is refreshing. Just as refreshing is Peake's elegant, direct prose. 'If the following pages sound didactic through lack of elbow room,' he tells us, 'it must be stressed at once that every hard and fast rule, here or elsewhere, is made to be broken.'

The pamphlet runs to a concise nineteen pages and is illustrated by Peake's own pencil drawings. They wonderfully encapsulate the points he makes, from the broodingly expressive portrait of a girl lit from below, to a sinuous life drawing of a female nude which shows how a line's 'rhythm' can bring a drawing to life. Headings such as 'Clumsiness', 'How to Stare', 'Expressiveness', 'Proportion' and 'Rhythm' take the reader swiftly through the rudiments of drawing and are punctuated by wonderful *bons mots*.

'Neither be afraid of the unorthodox subject nor in finding delight in the contemplation of commonplace things. Anything, seen without prejudice, is enormous,' Peake writes in his introduction. Of the lead pencil he writes, 'For the pianist his keyboard. For the writer his vocabulary. For the draughtsman a stick of graphite . . . a soft pencil ranges from the frailest of greys to the black of the tomb. Hell and Heaven in a cedar tunnel.' On drawing, Peake tells us to 'stare long and hard . . . Your hand must follow and not precede your idea.' 'The secret is to draw with intelligence, to be sure of what you want; for if you are undecided, so will your drawing be.' 'Make drawings every day,' he advises. 'If you have no paper, make them mentally, as though your brain had become your pencil-point.' Wonderful advice, beautifully illustrated by Peake's own drawings. My favourite advice is, 'Do not be afraid to exaggerate in order to convey the real intention of your drawing', which is music to a cartoonist's ears.

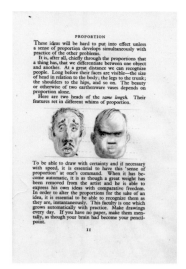

What *The Craft of the Lead Pencil* does so well is to confront the tyranny of the blank sheet of paper. It answers the questions any would-be draughtsman faces – 'What shall I draw? What am I trying to convey? And how best can I convey it?' Peake does this simply and elegantly by introducing the reader to 'a new way of looking', something he describes as 'the way for a draughtsman'. One only has to look at Peake's thoughtful, funny, poignant drawings to see that when he writes about the craft of the lead pencil he is a master craftsman. I have always loved drawing from as far back as I remember and was once asked what my idea of happiness was. I decided that happiness was a desk, a stove and an endless supply of paper and pencils. I could sit at the desk and draw endlessly, each completed drawing going into the stove to keep me warm. Peake ends *The Craft of the Lead Pencil* with these words:

'What does it matter how long or how slow you are in this traffic of lead and paper? The advance from virtual blindness to that state of perception – half rumination, half scrutiny – is all that matters. The end is hypothetical. It is the journey that counts.'

Amen to that.

Top
Four pages from *The Craft of the Lead Pencil* starting with the nude mentioned by Chris Riddell

Below
A match-seller sketched in the street

Learning the Craft

JOHN WOOD

Facing page
Sketches from the Central School
of Art

Top left
Cecil Collins

Bottom left
William Roberts

Top and bottom right
Models posing

Above
A man sketched during Peake's
visit to Spain in 1956

The main reason for my applying to be a student at the Central School of Arts and Crafts was that I had heard that Mervyn Peake taught life drawing there. I joined in the autumn of 1954, enrolled for the Tuesday class which he regularly took with Cecil Collins and waited agog for the morning when I should at last see what Mervyn Peake looked like.

I was not disappointed. Tall, dressed in a sports jacket and coloured shirt, with grey flannel trousers and black polished shoes; with large hands and a shock of greying hair, deep-set 'haunted' eyes and a sensitive, ascetic and masculine face, he seemed to be a throwback to the London Bohemia of the 1920s. He looked exactly the kind of person that could produce Peake drawings and Peake writings. His voice was a quiet, high tenor, with an audible intake of breath and a faintly querulous pitch to it.

Except for smoking a few cigarettes, he was inactive in the class until some drawing had been produced by the students. Cecil Collins usually set the model's pose, with Peake's approval. Then Peake walked along behind the row of donkey stools and, briefly scrutinizing the work done, selected a student to instruct. When my turn came to be the fortunate one, my heart beat faster. He stared at my drawing, muttered, 'I think I see what you're trying to do', and then, taking the pen between the joint of his right-hand thumb and forefinger, in silence, but with confidence – oh, such confidence – made the first marks in the margin of the paper.

In a few moments he had produced a brilliant line-drawing of the model's head. Then, taking a 2B pencil, he drew the head again, this time in bolder strokes, with the modelling and the shadows emphasized. He still said nothing . . . When he had drawn what he considered was sufficient Peake smiled in a way that was completely unpatronizing and turned his attention to another student.

It was always a joy to see him enter the life classes, quiet as a ghost, and melt into the background. I don't think that half the students knew who he really was, and it was rather saddening to see them sitting, looking languidly on, while he drew

Above
The 'Small Boy with Birdling'
given to Robin Wood

Above right
Pencil sketch of nude model

Facing page
Preparatory sketch for an
illustration to 'The Sphinx'
by Oscar Wilde

exquisite vignettes in the margins of their sketching boards. I remember on one occasion a girl student was so disgusted with her own work (whether by comparison with Mervyn's or not, I don't know) that she tore up the sheet, which included a marginal study by Mervyn, into inch-square fragments. After class I rescued them from the waste basket and carefully pieced them together. It was a full-length drawing, in line of great economy, of a seated nude, Marjorie Butler, who was a regular sitter. The necklace that she was wearing was treated with delicate, almost abstract, emphasis.

My most unforgettable encounter with Mervyn was when he invited me and my younger sister, Robin, to dinner one evening at a restaurant. After the meal, we walked, in the dusk, to Manresa Road. As we approached Trafalgar Studios, Mervyn indicated the unkempt façade: 'I warn you,' he said, 'this is chic compared to what it's like inside.' He unlocked the doors and led us in. It was a large room with big northern windows, but now the light had faded and the studio was filled with shadows. The place was in a state of picturesque disarray. On a large easel was pinned the cartoon for the Mocker in 'Christ and the Mockers'. On a table by the window stood two of Maeve's paintings. A small sepia-tinted photograph of someone in army uniform was pinned to the wall together with scribbled notes and sketches.

Mervyn produced a flat, narrow, half-imperial-sized suitcase, finished in grey cloth, and opened it. The drawings poured out: the Cat Studies, the Mouse Studies, Studies of Nudes, Heads of London – they were a myriad. 'Would you like to choose one each? I warn you, if I don't want to let a drawing go, I'll tell you. I'm very possessive,' he said with a smile. After a difficult and somewhat agonizing choice I decided on a drawing of a girl's head in line on Kent paper; he called it 'Square-Jawed Susie'. Robin selected one, another large line drawing of a small boy in a conical cap, with a funny, grotesque birdling perched on his wrist. Mervyn borrowed my fountain pen for the inscriptions, and I forgot to ask him for it back. It was by now getting late. Mervyn saw me and my sister off in Manresa Road and went back alone in darkness to his studio.

Left
'Square-Jawed Susie', 1958

Right
Model posing with towel at the Central School

Facing page
The King of J, from an alphabetical series of 'Kings' drawn in 1939

Clockwise from top left
The Kings of Z, R, and Y

Facing page
The King of I

7 Illustrator

G. PETER WINNINGTON

Only Peake could have produced drawings for Alice in Wonderland *whose characters can look those of Tenniel straight in the eye without the hint of a blush.* **Langdon Jones**

Facing page
Sita, from *Quest for Sita* by
Maurice Collis

Above
Mr Transportouse from *The Adventures of the Young Soldier in Search of the Better World* by
C. E. M. Joad

In his graphic work Peake employed a variety of media and techniques. Many early pieces, such as the 'Peacock Pie' series, were executed with a pen, but he also explored the potential of watercolour as well as the range of tone and expression that can be achieved with the pencil – 'Hell and Heaven in a cedar tunnel', as he put it. Formal art studies introduced him to oil painting, which he used to great effect in his portraits. Although he found it the most difficult medium, he could surpass himself when inspired, as in the pictures of glass-blowers at work. But the constant in Peake's *œuvre* is the quality of his line and his ability to create volume and space with a minimum of means.

From this point of view, his illustrations, both to his own writing and to works by others, fall into three main groups. In the first we find *Captain Slaughterboard Drops Anchor* (1939), *The Adventures of a Young Soldier* (1943), *Prayers and Graces* (1944), *Quest for Sita* (1946), *Mr Pye* (1953) and *Figures of Speech* (1954). For these works the illustrations are based on the single line, drawn with pen and ink, that outlines or silhouettes objects, without recourse to shading or cross-hatching. At its most spare and economical, as in *Quest for Sita* (see pp. 107–10), this continuous thin line endows the space that it encloses with an extraordinary sense of three-dimensional volume and weight. The figures have a sculpturesque fullness and roundness at the same time as an ethereal beauty. What is more, for all its plastic quality, this beauty has nothing of the cold perfection of marble. On the contrary, Peake's figures are warm-blooded creatures, personalities infused with feeling and humour – sardonic, satiric or ironic; they express his love and appreciation of human imperfection.

In some of these works he added texture to objects by means of further pen strokes, ranging from the lightest of stippled dots, through very short lines, to long, straight or curving, parallel lines. On many pages of *Captain Slaughterboard*, for instance, this texturing serves to establish the various planes, foregrounding the grain of wood, for instance, or the luxuriant vegetation of the Pink Island, against

The drawings on this and the facing page are from *The Adventures of the Young Soldier in Search of the Better World* by C. E. M. Joad

Top
The Young Soldier confronts the Red-tape Worm

Bottom
A procession of persons in flowing robes

the generous white space of the background. It also serves Peake's humour, for it highlights patches on clothes, holes in shoes and flower patterns in the pirates' bandannas, not to mention their tattoos. As all the lines are uniformly fine and very rarely cross each other, they generate a sense of openness that is perfectly in keeping with the setting of the story on tropical seas and islands. The labour must have been prodigious: just one double spread, such as the scene depicting the crew of the Black Tiger pursuing the Yellow Creature (reproduced on pp. 124–5), involves thousands of tiny dots and strokes. And as Peake was a perfectionist in these matters the final version was the result of numerous attempts. One blotched line meant starting anew.

The second group of Peake's illustrations is characterized by cross-hatching. In *Ride a Cock-Horse* (1940), *The Hunting of the Snark* (1941), *All This and Bevin Too* (1943), *The Rime of the Ancient Mariner* (1943), *Alice's Adventures in Wonderland* and *Though the Looking-Glass* (1946) and (his crowning achievement) *Treasure Island* (1949), the lines of shading cross and combine to produce a range of tones that go from cobweb lightness to almost total darkness. So neat and careful are these lines that some people have mistaken the illustrations in *The Ancient Mariner*, for instance, for engraving. In Peake, we have Doré and the Dalziel brothers in one.

From Peake's preliminary sketches for these illustrations (some of which are reproduced in the following pages), it is clear that these tonal values were most important to him. In addition to making sketches with a pencil, he used water-colour washes to determine just how light or dark areas of the final picture should be. This concern continued after he had made his final cross-hatched drawing. When he received a proof of *Treasure Island*, he complained that one of the illustrations was 'too dark' – 'much darker than the original'– and instructed the publisher to 'make the whole picture fainter'. So while the overall effect may be reminiscent of engraving, Peake was concerned that his pictures should not be too gloomy.

He also achieved dramatic effects by drawing long parallel lines for the background. Sometimes they fan out, as in the superb full-length portrait of Long John Silver (p. 123), and sometimes they curve and swirl, as in the equally memorable depiction of the fall of Israel Hands (p. 121). In the first case, they give tremendous energy to a static body; in the second they convey the stomach-churning, dizzying sensation of a downward plunge. In *The Craft of the Lead Pencil* Peake exaggerates his technique to show lines moving left and right. In the published books, the technique is invisible and the impact total. As with the first group, all these pictures demonstrate Peake's uncanny sense of the outline of figures, without which these background lines would be meaningless.

However, in many of the illustrations of this second group, the outline itself is in fact absent. Having pencilled in the silhouette, Peake drew shading round it, leaving white space instead of the line. This technique can be most clearly seen at work in the depiction of the crew of the *Hispaniola* gazing at treasure island by moonlight (p. 122). Inverting values like this makes the subjects stand out powerfully against the cross-hatched background. Peake also used it for features within foregrounded objects, drawing the shadows (folds of clothing, for instance) and leaving the highlights untouched. In the picture of Long John Silver pulling a rope with his teeth (p. 123), a seam running down the sleeve his shirt is so three-dimensional that one feels it must be raised from the surface of the paper. The eye is fooled into seeing a line that is not there, for the seam is in fact white space. Peake's illustrations to *Treasure Island* gain much of their effect from this technique.

Whereas the works of the first group are original, most of the second group are classics, with a long history of illustration behind them. The difference in Peake's technique reflects his response to his great predecessors: Rowlandson, Cruikshank, Bewick, Palmer, Leach, Hogarth, Blake, Doré, Grandville, Dürer and Goya (the list is his). He studied and acknowledged their work in his own illustrations, not only in his evocation of nineteenth-century engraving but also by echoing them in his compositions, perspective, framing devices and depicted gestures. His illustration to the title page of the first chapter of *Treasure Island*, for instance, shows a pirate about to throw a knife. That knife, balanced in the outstretched palm, pays homage to a scene in N. C. Wyeth's famous edition of the book. Similarly, the view of Jim firing two pistols down from the mast at Israel Hands is also from Wyeth. I call this homage, for there is nothing derivative about the way in which Peake uses his predecessors. As he put it, the illustrator is like 'a prince who with a line of kings for lineage can make no gesture that does not recall some royal ancestor'.

Household Tales (1946), containing a mix of plain line and and cross-hatching, falls between these two groups. It's a personal interpretation of an established classic. It also contains instances of a variation on Peake's basic technique: to create the softer silhouette of an animal's coat or fur (or the stubble of man's unshaved chin), he places numerous very short strokes at right-angles to the outline (see pp. 126–9). Again, its success depends on Peake's fine sense of the shape of humans and animals.

For this reason, when Peake undertook to illustrate a book, he devoted much time and attention to finding not just satisfactory compositions for the pictures but also the right postures and attitudes for the characters. This can be seen in the many preliminary sketches he made for *The Hunting of the Snark*, for instance (pp. 111–15), and for *Bleak House* (pp. 142–8), a contract that unfortunately fell through before completion. (Worse, after Peake's sketches were first published in 1983 all but the larger, more finished plates disappeared.) The sketches also show the care Peake took to depict historically correct details of clothing and context, as he did, too, for *Witchcraft in England*.

Works in the third group of Peake's illustrations were executed with a brush rather than the pen. Here we can distinguish a first series, comprising *Rhymes Without Reason* (1944) and *Witchcraft in England* (1945), painted before Peake was given some Chinese brushes by his father at the end of 1946, and those that followed, 'drawn' with a brush: *Dr Jekyll and Mr Hyde* (1948), *The Swiss Family*

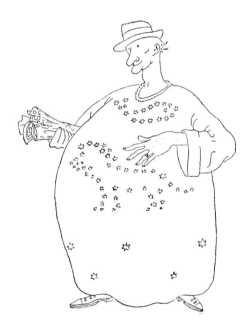

Top
The devices on the robes of the Oxford Groupers depicted men climbing the masts of ships and attaching various soiled garments to them

Bottom
On the robes of the Astrologers appeared heavenly constellations and signs of the Zodiac: lions, fishes and virgins

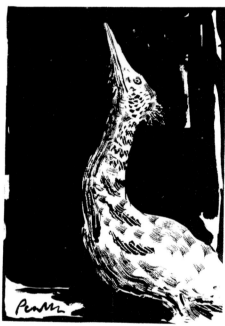

Two illustrations to poems by
Oscar Wilde

Top
Old Pan for 'The Garden of Eros'

Bottom
The 'gaunt bittern' among the
reeds for 'Humanitad'

Robinson (1949) and the series of illustrations to poems by Oscar Wilde, executed in the late 1940s but not published until 1980. What is striking about Peake's illustrative work with the Chinese brush is the extent to which he used it more like a pencil, producing sumptuous lines and curves rather than wider areas of continuous tone.

The brush lends itself to colour, of course, but colour printing was complicated and costly in Peake's time, so few of his illustrated works contain it. (See his contributions to *Lilliput* on pp. 132–3, which date from the early 1950s.) In *Rhymes without Reason*, Peake's book of nonsense for children (pp. 130–1), the publisher gave him a chance to let himself go, and he produced a series of garish pictures of the kind that children love. (One critic described the book as having the appearance of 'a sort of flagseller's night out'. Quite what that would be, I don't know, but it is obviously not intended as a compliment.) In *Witchcraft in England* (pp. 134–7) Peake combined all his techniques: plain line for some drawings, dark cross-hatching for others and pen and wash in yet others. It is all the more unfortunate that the plates executed with a brush should have been purloined from the publisher's archives, making it impossible for us to appreciate this work in a new edition using modern printing techniques.

With these illustrations, Peake acquired an uneasy reputation for producing pictures that were grotesque and macabre. The portrait of Life-in-Death (p. 151) that he drew for *The Rime of the Ancient Mariner* was rejected. He told John Wood that 'the publishers thought that it would be unfair to the general public to have them buy the book and then come across a picture like that when turning the pages. It had to come out.' This did not prevent it from being shamelessly plagiarized by a commercial artist, who had seen it in reproduced in *Poetry London* X (1944) and *Designers in Britain*, for the dust-wrapper of *The Hounds of Tindalos* (1950). This reputation led to commissions like *Thou Shall Not Suffer a Witch* (1949), simply on the grounds that Peake was the man for such a theme, which merely reinforced the prejudice. John Wood reports that in the mid-1950s 'he told me that he was doing some drawings that were going to be used as illustrations for a story in *Lilliput* about the aftermath of a nuclear war. Regretfully, he later said: "They thought the drawings were too horrible. They couldn't print them. But", he added, with a comforting smile, "I got paid." Eventually, the story appeared, illustrated by a competent though highly inferior artist: the result was slick and disappointing.'

Dramatic proof of Peake's skill in dealing with horrifying stories is supplied by the illustrations he made for *Dr Jekyll and Mr Hyde* (pp. 138–41). There he used his Chinese brush with great dexterity, combining his eye for line with his skill in the use of shadow. The preliminary sketches for the frontispiece show him combining a lamp sketched in a London street with various stances of a grotesque, hunched figure beneath it to generate verisimilitude in the fantastic, a visual correlate to his verbal inventions in the Titus books. What holds them all together, words and images alike, is his exquisite sense of shape.

In Search of Gormenghast

JOHN HOWE

When I was about Steerpike's age, I clambered up a ladder of ivy and through an attic window into Gormenghast. The climb was entirely motivated by a fellow student (who has gone on to become one of Canada's prominent voices in poetry); he would occasionally, and with authority, thrust books under my nose and say, 'Read this!'

'But what is it?' I asked.

'Read it. You'll find out,' he replied. And added cryptically, 'Maybe.'

Thus, I owe Mervyn Peake a life-long fascination with windy towers and walls of crumbling stone. I owe him the Gothic yearning for extravagant perpendiculars, an infatuation with horizons, an undeniable tenderness for the grotesque. Curiously enough, I only discovered Peake's illustrations much later. His texts stoked such a raging fire of imagination that I missed the connection between the exquisite portraits on the covers and the author. Enamoured of the author, I overlooked the artist. Since then I have read nearly everything available by and about Mervyn Peake and sought out his extraordinary images wherever I can, my penance for being born too late to meet the man.

Where is Gormenghast? When is Gormenghast? What is it? And, more importantly, how can I get there? When setting out on a journey, a step in any direction will do. So I enrolled in a college in France, since there was little likelihood Gormenghast would be nestled in the Rockies or tucked away in the outskirts of Vancouver, Chicago or San Francisco. It was obvious enough that the stone for Gormenghast must have been cut from some cyclopean European quarry, so I came to the Old World in 1976, intending to stay a year. The search is taking longer than expected. But, then, grails are like that.

I truly believe that those illustrators who owe a debt to Mervyn Peake are legion. Likely far more than any of us realize. Few other modern authors have opened up such a kingdom to wander in. Few authors have painted in such a vivid landscape, and fewer still have created a genre that they alone occupy. Peake paints

Above
Titus being carried to his tenth birthday masque, from the manuscript of *Gormenghast*

in words – emotions applied with a palette knife, characters detailed with the finest brush, atmosphere like a watercolour wash. There are no words that are right to describe Peake's words; only images will do. But when brush is applied to paper, when colours are chosen, architectures sketched out, Peake's world recedes into mist and shadow, into the realm of the possible and the imagined. Suddenly, any attempt at pigment on paper falls short. There's nothing for it, then; it requires sketches done *in situ*, deep in some windswept and ragged landscape of the mind. Whatever it is I am drawing, Mervyn Peake is there to urge me on.

In the end, Mervyn Peake's world is the invitation and the destination. Wantonly encouraging my bent for beauty askew, elegant decay and lines gone awry, and confirming, with every precious glimpse of Gormenghast, whether by chance or design, that the right path has been chosen.

Gormenghast is a state of mind, an angle of view, a passion for atmosphere and light. Gormenghast is random pages in a sketchbook, odd photographs with an unusual view, a trick of the light or a flaw in the lens. Gormenghast is views that turn out to be suddenly mundane from the wrong angle or when shared in the wrong company or sought out.

Luck affords brief glimpses of Gormenghast here and there – pine forests and ruins in the Vosges, towers in Tuscany and decaying mansions in the Piedmont or in Poland, roofscapes and attics in Le Puy-en-Velay, cemeteries in Paris or Prague.

Perhaps one day, I will have found it all, like the pieces of some vast puzzle without corners or edges. Then I will be standing on that spot where Titus stands at the end of *Titus Alone*, but it will be to set up an easel, not to turn and stride away.

IMAGE COURTESY OF UNIVERSITY COLLEGE LONDON

Right

The Mud Huts at the foot of the castle walls; a sketch from the manuscript of *Gormenghast*

Quest for Sita

In Maurice Collis's retelling of the
Sanscrit epic about how the
beautiful Sita is carried off by the
Dark Angel, there are no captions
to Mervyn Peake's drawings,
for (as here) they often do not
correspond to a specific character
or moment

Peake.

Facing page
Surpanakha begins a dance of
enticement and (above) turns
into an evil spirit.

Right
Sita

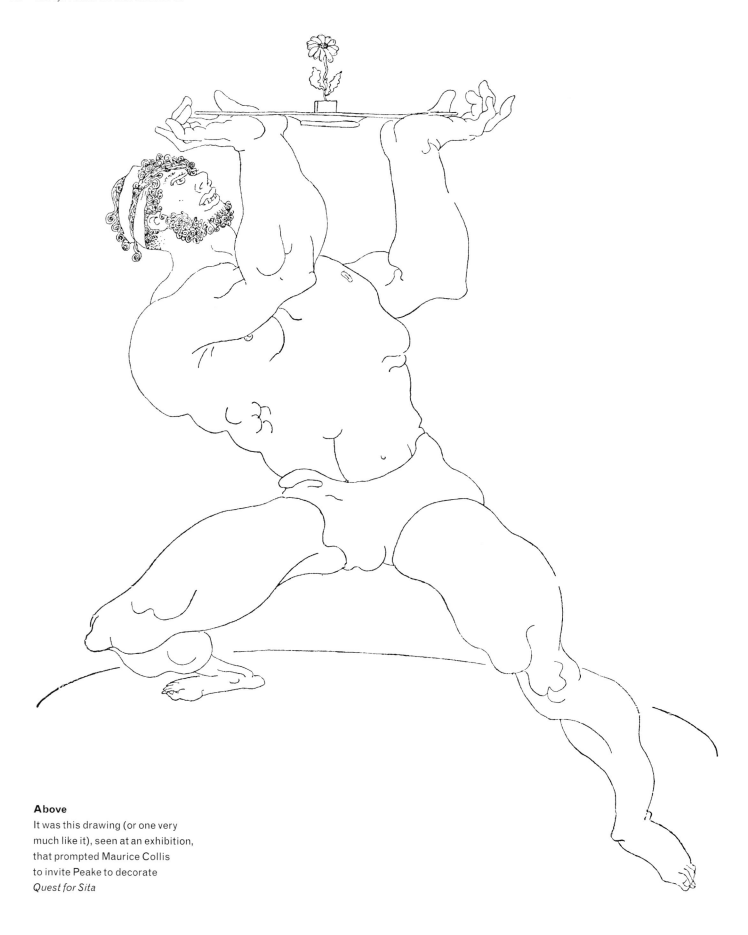

Above
It was this drawing (or one very
much like it), seen at an exhibition,
that prompted Maurice Collis
to invite Peake to decorate
Quest for Sita

The Hunting of the Snark

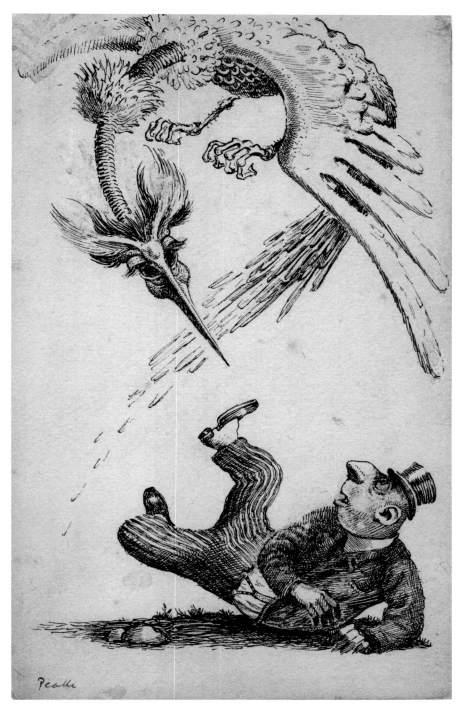

Above
The Bandersnatch attacks the Banker

Top right
The Barrister wakes 'to the knell of a furious bell, /Which the Bellman rang close to his ear'

Centre right
The Broker with a railway share

Bottom right
Charming it with smiles and soap

The Bellman

Facing page

Preliminary sketches for the Bellman

Right

Title page frame, also used on the original dust-wrapper

Facing page
Preliminary drawings for (top) the
Bellman stretched full length and
(bottom) the Billiard Marker
whistling for a Snark

Right
Preliminary sketches for the
Billiard Marker

Alice's Adventures in Wonderland

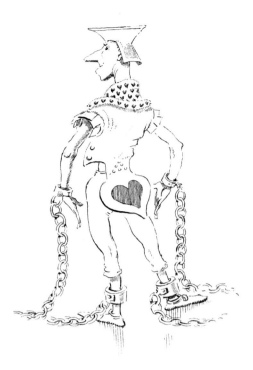

Characters from *Alice's Adventures in Wonderland* and *Through the Looking-Glass.* Restored drawings courtesy of the Libanus Press

Facing page

Top
'Alice went on growing and growing, and very soon had to kneel down on the floor'

Bottom left and right
The Lobster Quadrille and the three card-gardeners who were painting the roses

This page

Top left
The Knave of Hearts

Top right
The Frog footman delivering an invitation from the Queen

Bottom left
The Duchess

Bottom right
The Frog Footman

Top left
The Mouse calls out, 'Sit down all of you and listen to me'

Top right
The Dodo tries to think of the answer to the question

Bottom right
The Horse puts his head out of the carriage window

Facing page
The Messenger looks at Hatta as a tear or two trickles down his cheek

Treasure Island

Top left
Jim Hawkins caught by the pirates

Top right
Long John Silver cleaning his knife
on a wisp of grass after killing Tom

Bottom left
'The boarders swarmed over the
stockade like monkeys'

Bottom right
'Come, now, march!' Blind Pew
and Jim

Facing page
Israel Hands falls from the mast

Facing page

Top left
Jim Hawkins

Top right
'The Sea Cook': Long John Silver
with parrot

Bottom left
Abraham Gray with a knife-cut on
the side of his cheek

Bottom right
First sight of Treasure Island.
Mervyn Peake's notes for the
publisher on a proof

This page

Top left
Long John Silver. 'He was very tall
and strong, with a face as big as a
ham.'

Centre
In the treasure cave, 'packing the
minted money into bread bags'

Top right
Long John Silver drags Jim along

Bottom right
'The captain lying full length upon
the floor'

Captain Slaughterboard Drops Anchor

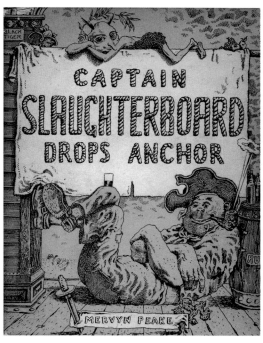

Left

The crew of the *Black Tiger* hunt for the Yellow Creature on its pink island; pen and ink

Above

The cover of the second edition of *Captain Slaughterboard Drops Anchor* (Eyre and Spottiswoode, 1945)

Household Tales
by the Brothers Grimm

Top left
The Queen Bee

Above and left
Cinderella

Facing page

Top left
One-Eye, Two-Eyes and Three-Eyes

Top right and bottom left
Snow White and the Seven Dwarfs

Bottom right
The Mouse, the Bird and the
Sausage

Top left and right
The Wolf and the Seven Little Kids

Above
The Little Peasant

Top left
The Singing Soaring Lark

Top right
The Three Spinners

Bottom left and right
The Turnip

Rhymes without Reason

In this volume, Peake illustrated his own nonsense poems. The dust-wrapper design and the illustrations of the elephant (below) and the giraffe (on the facing page) appeared only in the first edition, for they were subsequently lost.

How mournful to imagine

Our Ears, you know, have Other Uses,
    For, when we are dead,
The Coloured Pirates swarm ashore
    And chop them off one's head!

Far out at sea, beneath the stars
    They sew them into Sails,
So that their wicked ships can leap
    Among the Killer whales.

How mournful to imagine
    Our poor Ears being furled
By pirates in some purple bay
    Half-way across the world!

Overleaf
Two contributions to *Lilliput* magazine

Page 132
Four illustrations for nursery rhymes, May 1950

Page 133
'The Wendigo' by Algernon Blackwood, December [1951] –January 1952

The Giraffe

You may think that he's rather slow
    At seeing jokes, but O, dear no,
It isn't that at all, and I
    Will furnish you the reason why.

You see, with such a Normus Neck,
    It takes his laughter half a week
To climb so very far from where
    It started from, which isn't fair –

Because, when it has reached his face,
    He finds that he has *lost the place*,
And can't remember what was so
    Amusing half a week ago!

Sensitive, Seldom and Sad

Sensitive, Seldom and Sad are we,
As we wend our way to the sneezing sea,
With our hampers full of thistles and fronds
To plant round the edge of the dab-fish ponds;
O, so Sensitive, Seldom and Sad –
Oh, *so* Seldom and Sad.

In the shambling shades of the shelving shore,
We will sing us a song of the Long Before,
And light a red fire and warm our paws
For it's chilly, it is, on the Desolate shores,
For those who are Sensitive, Seldom and Sad,
For those who are Seldom and Sad.

Sensitive, Seldom and Sad we are,
As we wander along through Lands Afar,
To the sneezing sea, where the sea-weeds be,
And the dab-fish ponds that are waiting for we
Who are, Oh, so Sensitive, Seldom and Sad,
Oh, *so* Seldom and Sad.

Lilliput

Children's Hour

Four Nursery Rhymes Illustrated by

MERVYN PEAKE

With a Commentary by Leslie Daiken

IN 1837 a Mr. John B. Ker published a large volume, annotated up to the hilt, to prove that nursery rhymes were cryptic slogans against corruption in the Church.

Since then, countless other experts—ethnologists, philologists, musicologists, historians and preachers—have followed in his footsteps, and come to widely divergent conclusions of their own.

They have had a fertile field in which to work, for nursery lore contains something like 600-odd snippets, which can be said to pass for rhymes. Yet only a fraction of them are true children's doggerel. The rest stem from a grown-ups' world—shreds of rural malice, old folk-fancies, libellous lampoons, political satire grown blunt, miniatures of history, or lullabies devised by harassed mothers.

These four nursery rhymes, illustrated by Mervyn Peake, have as complex a background as any.

The first one—'How many miles to Babylon?'—is cast in the mould of a parley between travellers and the Gate Keeper of some ancient walled city. This, no doubt, will come as a surprise even to the brightest child.

The parley was used as a rhyme accompaniment to a game similar to 'Oranges and Lemons,' but what walled cities have to do with oranges or lemons has never been revealed. It may be accepted, however, that Babylon, in the nursery, represents the most remote of remote and mysterious places. In some nurseries it has become corrupted to 'Babyland,' while in Belfast it is known as 'Sandy Row'!

Where Babylon stands for a land of fantasy, Gotham is the town of fools. Early in the 16th century a Dr. Andrew Borde wrote some disagreeable stories about the Fools of Gotham; the rhyme about the three wise men in the bowl perpetuates their foolishness. There is a village near Leicester called Gotham, but this seems to be merely an unfortunate coincidence.

36

(*Continued on page* 41)

" How many miles to Babylon ? "
" Three score miles and ten."
" Can I get there by candle-light ? "
" Yes, and back again.
    If your heels are nimble and light
    You may get there by candle-light."

Hark ! Hark ! The dogs do bark,
The beggars are coming to town.
Some in rags and some in tags,
And some in silken gown.
Some gave them white bread,
And some gave them brown,
And some gave them a good horse-whip,
And sent them out of town.

(Continued from page 36)

LILLIPUT

The queen visited by the cat in the third picture is popularly supposed to have been Good Queen Bess. But the rhyme, 'Pussy-cat, pussy-cat, where have you been . . .' did not appear in print until 1805. It seems strange that the cat found no more immediate biographer, after having taken the trouble to walk all the way to London to see the Queen. Some doubt must be cast upon Elizabeth's part in the matter.

With the last picture, 'Hark, hark, the dogs do bark . . .', we seem to be on firmer ground, in possession of no less than two reasonable explanations of why the dogs did bark, and the beggars came to town.

Iona and Peter Opie, two inexhaustible researchers into the origins of nursery rhymes, maintain that this was a parody of a political song printed in 1672. Can it be a day at William of Orange, and Mary, his Queen, who arrived in England round about this time attended by a horde of singularly impecunious followers?

Some in rags and some in tags,
And some in a silken gown.

The fact that the song was written several years before William and Mary arrived in England can be explained by the theory that the writer had previously been to Holland, and, having seen the Dutch court, knew what to expect.

The other explanation has been provided by a Mr. A. B. Haigh. He provides a summary of social upheaval in the reign of Henry VIII.

"Britain," he says, "had turned over from arable to pastoral farming. Land workers wandering round the country were joined by manservants from the big feudal households, which had been broken up by Henry's Statute of Livery and Maintenance. The influx of these men without a trade worried town-people."

Some gave them white bread,
And some gave them brown,
And some gave them a good horse-whip,
And sent them out of town.

It is to be regretted, of course, that one nursery rhyme should have two such convincing, but diametrically opposed, explanations, since it leaves us in almost as great a state of uncertainty as before. But we have the comfort of knowing that there is always 'Ring-a-ring-a-roses,' the one nursery rhyme with a really solid historical background.

'Ring-a-ring-a-roses' is a song of the Great Plague. Here, everything fits beautifully into place.

The rings of roses are the plague spots. A pocketful of posies refers to the nosegays of herbs that people carried in the hope that the herbs would lend them immunity to the disease. And, 'Atishoo—atishoo—we all fall down!' is what happened when people found that the herbs didn't.

It might, at first sight, seem strange that so many little children, in these days, should derive so much innocent pleasure from gambolling about hand in hand singing cheerfully of a pestilence that swept their ancestors away by the hundred thousand; but then we must remember that we are dealing with the nursery rhyme.

In the nursery rhyme there may be rhyme, but there certainly is never any reason.

G   41

Three wise men of Gotham
Went to Sea in a Bowl.
If the Bowl had been stronger,
My tale had been longer.

" Pussy cat, Pussy cat, where have you been ? "
" I've been to London to visit the Queen."
" Pussy cat, Pussy cat, what did you there ? "
" I caught a little mouse under the chair."

THE WENDIGO

by

ALGERNON BLACKWOOD

" The face was more animal than human, the features drawn about into wrong proportions, the skin loose and hanging . . . "

A CONSIDERABLE number of hunting parties were out that year without finding so much as a fresh trail; for the moose were uncommonly shy, and the various hunters returned to the bosoms of their respective families with the best excuses the facts or their imaginations could suggest. Dr. Cathcart, among others, came back without a trophy; but he brought instead the memory of an experience which he declares was worth all the bull-moose that had ever been shot. But then Cathcart, of Aberdeen, was interested in other things besides moose—amongst them the vagaries of the human mind. This particular story, however, found no mention in his book on *Collective Hallucination* for the simple reason (so he confided once to a fellow colleague) that he himself played too intimate a part in it to form a competent judgment of the affair as a whole.

Besides himself and his guide, Hank Davis, there was young Simpson, his nephew, a divinity student destined for the "Wee Kirk" (then on his first visit to Canadian backwoods), and the latter's guide, Défago. Joseph Défago was a French "Canuck" who had strayed from his native Province of Quebec years before, and had got caught in Rat Portage when the Canadian Pacific Railway was a-building; a man who, in addition to his unparalleled knowledge of woodcraft and bush-lore, could also sing the old *voyageur* songs and tell a capital hunting yarn into the bargain. He was deeply susceptible, moreover, to that singular spell which the wilderness lays upon certain lonely natures. and he loved the wild solitudes with a kind of romantic passion that amounted almost to an obsession. The life of the backwoods fascinated him—whence, doubtless, his surpassing efficiency in dealing with their mysteries.

On this particular expedition he was Hank's choice. Hank knew him and swore by him. He also swore at him, just as a pal might.

This, then, was the party of four that

Illustrations by Mervyn Peake

81

Witchcraft in England

IMAGE COURTESY OF CHRIS BEETLES GALLERY

IMAGE COURTESY OF CHRIS BEETLES GALLERY

Captions within quotation marks are from the book by Christina Hole.

Above
'Searching for Devil's marks'

Bottom right
A witch and her familiar

Top right
'Ruth Osborne floated at first, and Thomas Colley ran into the water to thrust her down with a stick'

Facing page
'A number of women gathered round a huge fire'

IMAGE COURTESY OF CHRIS BEETLES GALLERY

IMAGE COURTESY OF CHRIS BEETLES GALLERY

IMAGE COURTESY OF CHRIS BEETLES GALLERY

IMAGE COURTESY OF CHRIS BEETLES GALLERY

Top left
'Hopkins with a suspected witch'

Top right
Jennet Preston: 'She confessed
nothing, but this did not save her'

Bottom left
'Hatred as a motive for false
accusation of sorcery'

Bottom right
'Suspect'

Facing page
'More dreadful was the deliberate
use of the sacred service itself to
loosen evil forces'

Dr Jekyll and Mr Hyde

Preliminary sketches and (facing
page) finished frontispiece

Facing page

Top left and centre
Finished illustration and
preliminary sketch

Top right
Finished illustration

Bottom left
Finished illustration which was
printed reversed left-to-right in
the book

Bottom right
Finished illustration not printed in
the book

This page

Top left and right
Finished illustrations

Bottom left and right
Preparatory sketches

Bleak House

Left, top and bottom
Mr Guppy

Top right
Mr Chadband

Bottom right
Jo the crossing-sweeper

Facing page
Lady Dedlock

Top
Preliminary and final illustrations
for Mrs Pardiggle and her brood

Bottom left
Judy Smallweed

Bottom right
Young Mr Smallweed

Facing page
Mrs Guppy

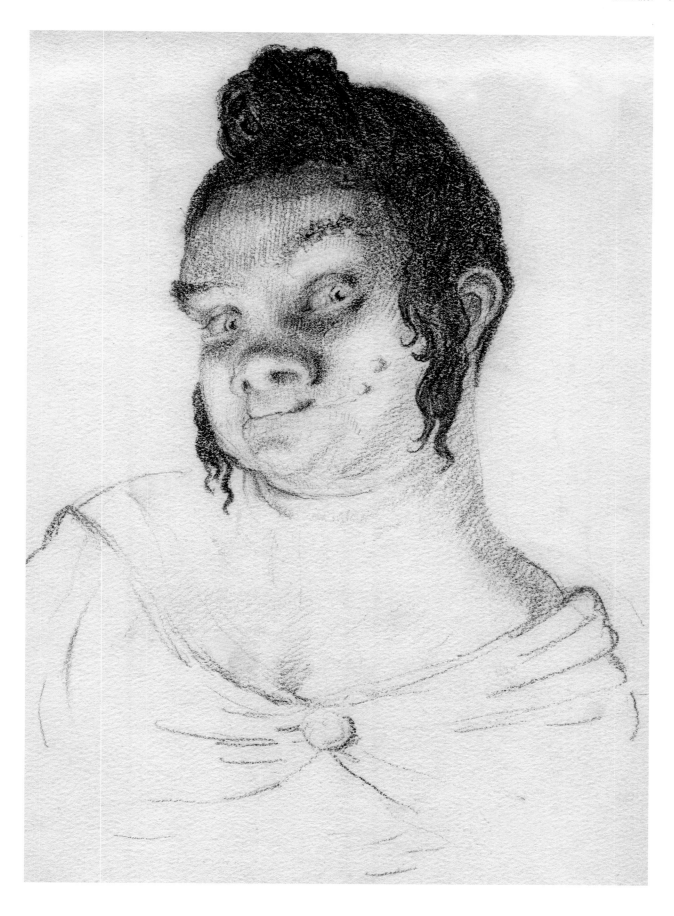

Above
Mr Vholes

Facing page, top left and right
Two studies of Harold Skimpole

Bottom left
Mr Gridley

Bottom right
Mr Snagsby

Top left
Miss Flite

Bottom left
Mr Turveydrop

Right
Unidentified character,
possibly Krook

Phantasmagoria

Two drawings for
'Phantasmagoria'
by Lewis Carroll

The Rime of the Ancient Mariner

The quotations are from
Coleridge's poem.

Right
'Instead of the Cross, the
Albatross/About my neck
was hung'

Facing page

Top left
'I pass, like night, from land to land'

Bottom left
'The sails did sigh like sedge'

Right
'The Night-mare Life-in-Death
was she.'

Top left

The crew see the phantom ship
against the western sun

Above

'With my cross-bow /
I shot the Albatross'

Bottom left

'The dead men stood together /
All fixed on me their stony eyes'

Facing page

The Ancient Mariner

8 Mr Pye

G. PETER WINNINGTON

*Mr Pye is an agreeable confection . . . a witty debate about good and evil [which]
underlines the innate comedy behind the inevitable seriousness of that perennial conflict.
It is a beguiling and delightful book which I enjoyed enormously.*　**Dominic Le Foe**

Facing page

Top
Mr Pye contemplates his mission
while sitting on one of the
Napoleonic cannons on Sark

Bottom
Ka-Ka prepares lunch

Above
Mr Pye catching his first view
of Sark

In 1953 Mervyn Peake published *Mr Pye*, a novel set on his beloved island of Sark.
It's the only work of his that describes a real place in detail, with characters whom
the Sarkese will happily identify for you, which makes it all the more surprising
when the story proves to be a flight of fantasy (in more than one sense). Mr Pye is a
portly little evangelist who attempts to convert the islanders to his own naïve brand
of Christianity. He rapidly transforms his landlady, a stiff-backed spinster named
Miss Dredger, into a disciple but fails to melt the heart of her arch-enemy, Miss
George. As his crusade progresses, the goodness in Mr Pye manifests itself in wings
that sprout from his shoulderblades. Finding these incongruous, he discovers that he
can make them diminish by deliberate acts of evil. But then he starts to grow horns,
which results in a quite literal struggle to find a balance between good and evil. The
resolution (which I will save for readers to discover for themselves) is both logical
and surprising. Those who are misled by the realism of the setting are generally
puzzled by this tale. Like the Titus books *Mr Pye* does not fit into any known genre.

Peake provided superb line drawings, executed with a felt pen, for the chapter
headings, and they contribute to this blurring of the borders between fact and
fiction. By depicting recognizable scenes – the cliffs, the harbour, the main street
and the rooftops of Sark with their characteristic witches' seats projecting from the
chimneystacks – he further anchors the story in the known world at the same time
as underlining the whimsy of his invention.

Mr Pye is full of irony and wit, much funnier than the Titus books. It is also
more deliberately patterned and worded than they are, showing that when he
wished to Peake could structure his writing with the same rigour that he brought
to his drawing. Not least among the ironies is the portrayal of the eponymous
evangelist. Coming from the pen of the son and grandson of Christian missionaries
to places such as China and Madagascar, *Mr Pye* questions their claim to a spiritual
truth which they sought to pass on to the natives. It is a personal reflection on the
nature of good and evil.

Less immediately, it is also about the relationships between art and religion and art and the world of commerce. Mr Pye would have the island's resident artist, Thorpe, who is for ever in search of the ultimate painting, believe that all inspiration is spiritual and divine. Thorpe finds it in the material world, for he is infatuated by the beauty of the island's whore, Tintagieu. That each exploits beauty in their respective trades is underlined when he tells her that she ought to be a film actress. 'They'd shoot you from below. Streamers of cloud behind your head and all that racket.' 'Shoot me from below? I'd like to see them,' retorts Tintagieu. 'Sounds bloody painful to me.' This exchange leads naturally into a splendid tirade, which Peake placed in Thorpe's mouth, linking all the themes of art and inspiration, artists and their physical suffering, the art trade and belief in spiritual values.

Above

A large grey goat: 'Its face was long enough for wisdom in all conscience. As for its eyes, Solomon sat in one of them, and Confucius in the other' (p. 179)

Right

Mr Pye addresses Miss George.

The Business of Art

FROM *MR PYE*

'Oh, these *theories*,' Thorpe added in a voice of scorn and with a flourish of his free arm (for Mr Pye still held the elbow of the other) – 'these theories about Art, they are all absolute n-nonsense.' (He was winding himself up, for Tintagieu was listening – he hoped.) 'Can't you see the whole thing is an organized racket? The p-painter digs his heart up and tries to sell it. The heart specialists become interested, for the thing is still b-beating. The hangers-on begin to suck the blood. They lick each other like c-cats. They bare their fangs like d-dogs. The whole thing is pitiful. Art is in the hands of the amateurs, the Philistines, the racketeers, the Jews, the snarling women and the raging queers to whom Soutine is "ever so pretty" and Rembrandt "ever s-so sweet".

'What do the galleries know? They are merely m-merchants. They sell pictures instead of lampshades and that's the only difference. And the critics – Lord, what clever b-boys they are! They know about everything except painting. That's why I came out here to get away from it all. The jungle of London with its millions of apes. I came out here to find myself, but have I done so? No, Mr Pye. Of c-course I haven't. For artists need competition and the stimulus of other b-brains whether they like it or not. They must talk painting, b-breathe painting, and be c-covered with paint. That is the kind of man I would talk to. A man c-covered with paint. And with paint in his hair and paint in the brain and on the b-brain – but where are they, these men? – they're in the great cities, among the m-monkeys where they can see each other work and fight it out, while as f-far as the public is concerned they might as well be knitting, or blowing b-bubbles, for even you, Mr Pye, if you don't mind my saying so, haven't got a c-clue to what it's all about, as your ridiculous "slap it on", "whisk it off", and "hey presto" attitude shows all t-too clearly. Your idea about colours is "the m-more the b-better", and "bright as p-possible", like a herbaceous b-border. Colour, Mr Pye, is a process of elimination. It is the d-distillation of an attitude. It is a credo.'

Mr Pye's face was pink with admiration. He ran his eyes over the painter as though he had never seen him before. He turned his head quickly to Tintagieu as though for corroboration and then he ran his eyes again all over Thorpe. 'That was superb,' he whispered, as though to himself.

From top

The virginal Miss Dredger clutches the sheets in alarm

Thorpe, the painter, trips and falls headlong into a rock pool

The chimney down which Miss George is lowered

Peake

Facing page

Top
Miss Dredger awaits the arrival of
Mr Pye at the old Creux harbour

Bottom left
Thorpe and Tintagieu

Bottom right
At the harbour wall

This page

Right
Cats on a Sark roof with traditional
witches' seats set into the chimney

Above
Tintagieu walks home, stark naked

9 The Art of Mervyn Peake

G. PETER WINNINGTON

The finest examples of any master's work . . . are compelling because they are not 'classic' and because they are not 'romantic'. They are both and they are neither. They are balanced upon a razor's edge between the passion and the intellect, between the compulsive and the architectonic. Out of this fusion there erupts that thing called 'style'. **Mervyn Peake**

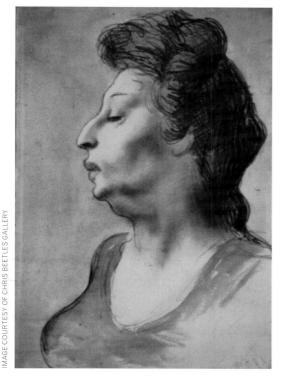

Facing page
Self-portrait, Sark, 1933

Above
Miss Greek, who frequently modelled
in London art schools during the 1940s.
Pencil and wash, first published in *The
Drawings of Mervyn Peake* (1949)

We all know beauty when we see it, although we may not always agree with other people on what they find beautiful. Mervyn Peake was born with the magic gift that turns an ordinary person into an artist: he could not only see beauty, he could create it on paper and canvas. What makes his work so special is his intense awareness of the borderline between beauty and ugliness. He knew from everyday experience how small the difference is between the line that describes a perfect curve and the line that fails. A millimetre too long, too short, too close, too fat, or too thin, and a limb of the human body or a feature of the face falls short of perfection and brings us up against our essential humanity. For it is not in human nature to be perfect and certainly not perfectly beautiful. In Peake's first presentation of Fuchsia in *Titus Groan* he describes her as 'in a sense, ugly of face, but with how small a twist might she not suddenly have become beautiful'. It's that twist, of feature as of fate, that marks Peake's life and art.

It's there is his earliest works. In a cartoon signed 'Nemo' he drew a lecturer standing before an audience of grotesques saying, 'It will be my endeavour, ladies and gentlemen, to convince you of the miraculous beauty of the human body!' To one side stands an armless classical statue, confirming that such beauty may exist in art but not in life. It also underlines another irony of fate: even our greatest works of art are liable to damage and destruction, truncated by time, cut off in their prime. So while Peake was clearly attracted to the beauty that he could create, the realist in him led him to depict his fellow men and women as they are. Seeing the borderline between the ideal and the real, he would exaggerate it, so that we have no choice but to see it, too. Thus his work tends towards the grotesque, as he celebrates our shortcomings.

Head-hunting: quick sketches, dating from the 1940s, of interesting faces glimpsed in the street. For lack of a notepad, Peake would draw on anything – paperbags and cigarette packets.

Drawings from 'London Fantasy',
published in *World Review*, 1949

Further sketches from the 1940s, in various media, of London figures, including two men in the Sports Drome, a slot machine arcade in the Tottenham Court Road

That playful humour saved him from despair. For all his observation of our defects, there is no bitterness in his world view. His commissioned portraits show rather tender compassion. As for those whom he caught unawares, sketched on his 'head-hunting' expeditions in the streets of London, or in the pubs and cafés that he frequented with his fellow artists, or wherever he went on the Continent, he treated them, too, with respect – just as long as they showed no exaggerated sense of self-importance. The society hostess (see p. 172) and the supercilious snob he could deflate with a flick of his brush. At these moments there's a satirist and even a moralist at work in Peake.

He did not spare himself. The face we see in his self-portraits often differs markedly from the one that looks out of photographs. There may be very good reasons for this. To start with, we do not see ourselves as the camera (or another person) sees us. Then, the mirror provides artists with a model who is infinitely patient and present. Whenever they are ready to paint, the sitter is ready, too. The young Rembrandt used his mirror frequently, pulling faces at himself to study the effect of emotion on his features and then etching what he saw. I suspect that in Peake's self-portraits (especially the one with his head thrown back and eyes wide, reproduced

Above
Two more trophies of Peake's 'head-hunting', a man in a bar and a boy in the street, in pencil and wash

More head-hunting

Top left
A waiter in Soho; chalks

Top right
Street market; chalks

Bottom left and right
Men in bars; mixed media

Facing page

Top right
Watching her undress (1956)

Bottom left
From *Quest for Sita*

Bottom right
Reclining figure

on p. 30) he was doing much the same thing. His posture certainly recalls a well-known self-portrait by Rembrandt. (Is it only coincidence that six months after Maeve gave birth to their first son and called him Sebastian, Peake produced a fictional son and called him Titus, the same name as Rembrandt's son?) Yet there was little vanity in Peake, only a humble awareness of his immense abilities, so that even his self-portraits verge on the grotesque.

In some people's mouths, the term 'grotesque' is an insult, yet it started life as an adjective to describe the late Roman art discovered around 1500 in the underground passages (or grottoes) of the baths of Titus – another one! In those murals and sculptures garlands intertwine with strange animal figures, so the term is quite apposite for Peake's work; he often played with human and animal forms. In his occasional sketches, in the doodles he made in the margins of his manuscripts, he would juxtapose a man and a beast, as though to remind himself (and us) that though we be animals, too, we are so much less beautiful than they. And to the animals he would give qualities (such as long eyelashes) that we find attractive in women. In some of his more careful drawings, like those for *Quest for Sita*, he juxtaposed a mythical beast and a beautiful woman and made their lines echo each other, especially the hips of the woman and the rump of the beast. The humour that deflates our sense of natural superiority is never far away. Perhaps this is why those who are uncomfortable with Peake's work are often those who take themselves rather seriously.

We find the same juxtaposition expressed in words when Peake portrays Keda, the girl from the Bright Carvers' mud huts, at the moment when the bane of her people is about to rob her of her beauty:

The dreadful and premature age that descended so suddenly upon the faces of the Dwellers had not yet completely fallen over her features. It was as though it was so close upon her that the beauty of her face cried out against it, defying it, as a stag at bay turns upon the hounds with a pride of stance and a shaking of antlers.

A hectic beauty came upon the maidens of the mud buildings a month or so before the ravages to which they were predestined attacked them. From infancy until this tragic interim of beauty their loveliness was of a strange innocence, a crystal-like tranquillity that held no prescience of the future.

This 'razor's edge' in Keda's life, poised between beauty and ugliness, expresses the essence of Peake's art: the depiction in word and image of ephemeral beauty threatened by time. The irony is that his works have the same innocence that holds 'no prescience of the future', for disease was to rob him of that very ability.

Peake was a great admirer of feminine beauty, yet he rarely exploits the erotic. His naked female figures have bodies that are poetic rather than provocative, for he sees shape before sex. And when he depicts a man looking at a naked woman he tends to downplay desire and desexualize the man, as in the monk-like figure watching a girl undress (p. 167). In *Witchcraft in England* and *Household Tales*, on the other hand, when men abuse their power over women he draws the victim from behind and makes us see, and reject, the lustful gaze of the men. Some of Peake's most erotic female figures are in the studies supposedly made by Hitler, and thus he points to the source of male violence against women.

In all these works, then, Peake manages to walk a tightrope, to maintain a subtle balance between beauty and ugliness. What really interested him was that invisible dividing line, that border between the two. In fact, we might even say that all Peake's work is about thresholds. In poetry he began (in 'The Touch 'o the Ash') with a captain who oversteps the mark and casts a sailor into the ship's furnace, and he ended (in *The Rhyme of the Flying Bomb*) with a sailor who saves a babe from the gutter and yet brings down a flying bomb upon himself. His stories are all about people who, in one way or another, cross a frontier of some kind. Captain Slaughterboard, who never goes on land, discovers love by leaving his ship and exploring the Yellow Creature's pink island. Titus Groan defiantly rides out of Gormenghast to go and discover the wide world beyond the confines of the castle. Peake's last (unfinished) work is about Footfruit's journey, accompanied by the dog that laughs like a drain, over the Border to the Great City and back again.

In his instructions to students, he advised them to pay attention to edges:

Do not try and get solidity. Solidity will come by paying lynx-like attention to the structure of the object, and by thinking of the shadows as results of that structure. The shadow graduates around the egg with no sharp edges. Why? Because, unlike the cube, the object has no sharp edges. The shadow is the result. The object's form, the cause.

IMAGE COURTESY OF CHRIS BEETLES GALLERY

Facing page
Grotesque head, first published in *The Drawings of Mervyn Peake* (1949)

Top
Image in oils

Above
Sad Creature, first published in *The Drawings of Mervyn Peake* (1949)

This leads him to conclude that 'There are no accidental shadows.' Indeed, because Peake's work is all about this interplay of light and darkness, of good and evil, of beauty and ugliness, and the razor's edge between them, there are no accidental shadows in his work.

'The ravages to which [he was] predestined' was a bitter twist of fate. Treated for Parkinson's disease with terrifying electric current therapy, he wrote to Maeve, 'I have played too much around the edge of madness.' Unsympathetic readers have emphasized the 'madness' in that statement. We can see that his cry expresses his life's work. From start to finish, he was playing around the edges, that invisible line that separates the 'madness' of the artist from that of the common man.

This page
Two London street figures from the 1940s

Facing page
Study of a woman's head, first published in *The Drawings of Mervyn Peake* (1949)

Overleaf

Page 172
The Hostess, first published in *The Drawings of Mervyn Peake* (1949)

Page 173
Two Men of London, 1947, first published in *The Drawings of Mervyn Peake* (1949)

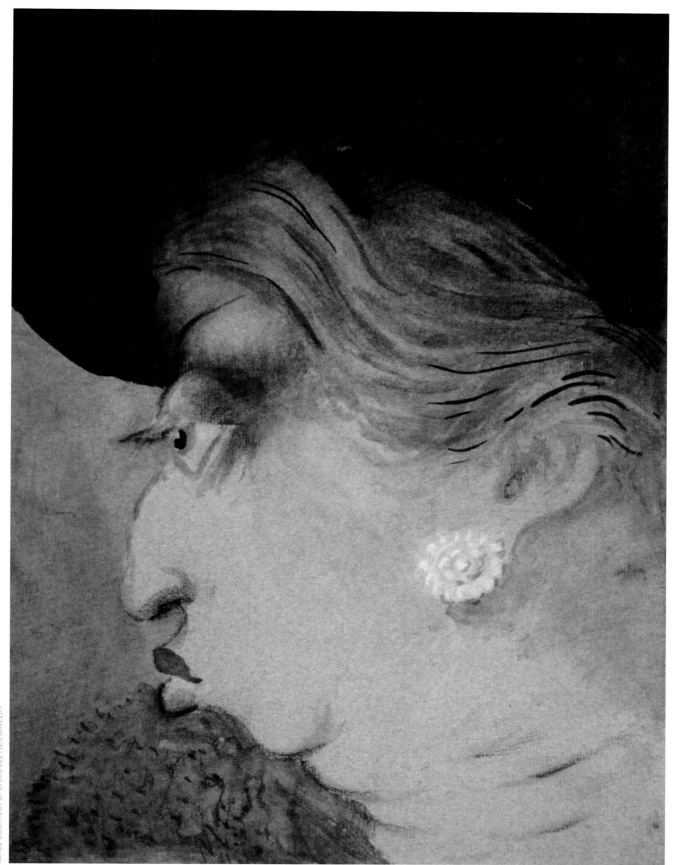

Top left
Full-length portrait in mixed media, 1939

Top right
Susan French, a family friend

Bottom left
Pamela Grove, pastel on toned paper, September 1950

Bottom right
Julie French

Facing page
Mervyn Peake's niece, Victoria Worthington, c.1950

10 Plays and Adaptations

These, the imponderable platforms: the breathless theatres.
What should we hope for as the curtain rises and lays bare the gratuitous stage
where, unhindered, a man may cry his ghostly manifesto? A miracle? Of course.

Mervyn Peake

Throughout the 1950s Peake wrote plays, starting with adaptations of *Titus Groan* and *Mr Pye* for the radio. Then he moved on to original stage plays like *Anima Mundi or, The Cave* and *Noah's Ark*. Ironically, the latter has so far been performed only as a radio play. In it a boy falls asleep while playing with his ark and dreams that he is back with Noah. Peake drew costumes for several of the animal characters, who could be played by children.

He wrote and rewrote numerous versions of his verse comedy, *The Wit to Woo*, which was finally had a brief run at the Arts Theatre, London, in the spring of 1957. Percy Trellis loves Sally Devius, the daughter of the eccentric, bed-ridden Old Man Devius. Unfortunately, Percy finds himself tongue-tied in the presence of Sally, yet he has no problem with his lines as an amateur actor. So he fakes his suicide and returns at his own funeral in the guise of his imaginary cousin, the artist October Trellis. Sally is impressed by him but would have preferred the old Percy. Meanwhile, her father has turned out to be bankrupt and bailiffs remove all his furniture. In the empty house, Percy reverts to his old self and at first is taken for a ghost. When he finally wins Sally, she gets both the old Percy and his flamboyant cousin in one. Despite the care that Peake lavished on it, the play remains flawed, torn between its flimsy plot and its flowery language.

Since Peake's death, there have been several adaptations of his work. One year *Titus Alone* was dramatized by Oxford students and went on to the Edinburgh Fringe. *Mr Pye* was made into a Channel 4 television drama, starring Derek Jacobi, and the story of Titus at Gormenghast has inspired both a stage production by the David Glass Ensemble and a mini-series for BBC television.

Facing page
Four costume designs for
Noah's Ark, a play for children

SALLY DEVIUS

    O have a heart!

GUISEPPE

    I have little else. I am all heart. It is too big for me.
    My ribs are aching with the size of it.

Act II.

page 29.

Characters from Peake's play,
The Wit to Woo

Facing page
Giuseppe (who became October
Trellis in the performed and
published version of the play)

Top left
Percy Trellis as Giuseppe

Top right
Percy as himself

Bottom left
Dr Willy and Giuseppe

Bottom right
Kite and Percy Trellis

Top left
Sally Devius

Top right
Dr Willy

Bottom
Old Man Devius descends to
the stage in his bed, watched
by Giuseppe and Dr Willy

Facing page

Top
The four undertakers; watercolour

Bottom left
Dr Willy

Bottom centre
Old Man Devius wearing his top
hat in bed

Bottom right
The four undertakers; pen and ink

THE FOUR UNDERTAKERS (singing)

" To our primordial calling
We bring both craft & grace –
We know our place...."

Act 1   page-5.

The Glass Gormenghast

JOHN CONSTABLE

Pages 182–8
Photographs of the 2006
David Glass production of
Gormenghast

Above
The Countess

In 1991 I was commissioned by the David Glass Ensemble to write the stage adaptation of Gormenghast – an enticing prospect, and quite daunting! Mervyn Peake's Gothic trilogy defies literal translation. No stage version can hope to recreate the visions he conjures in the reader's imagination. Peake created a sovereign world of the imagination, teeming with larger-than-life eccentrics and grotesques. As dramatist, my task was to reinvent his sprawling literary masterpiece in a stripped-down, character-driven narrative; to reflect the beauty and terror of that world and to reveal its resonance with our own.

The director David Glass and I agreed on the basic shape and style of the play: a melodrama charting the decline and fall of the House of Groan, Gormenghast's dysfunctional ruling family, and the journey to manhood of Titus, its son and heir. My close working relationship with David encouraged me to write to the strengths of the Ensemble. I juxtaposed key scenes of dramatic conflict with elemental images that drew on all the resources of physical theatre – Flay's journey through a labyrinth of passages and stairways to Swelter's hellish kitchen; the flood that engulfs the castle – confident that David's direction would rise to the challenge.

I reread the novels, without taking notes, then wrote down the scenes that stuck in my mind, mapping out a rough narrative structure. I compressed the epic sweep of *Titus Groan* into a highly stylized Act One, evoking Titus's nightmarish childhood. Acts Two and Three mine a relatively narrow vein of the second *Gormenghast* novel, focusing on the young man's rites of passage. A dream-fragment from *Titus Alone* inspired the final scene, in which Titus comes of age, renouncing his inheritance.

I wrote the play quickly, drawing freely on Peake's original dialogue as the text for a ritual drama, set in a world bound by iron laws and the dead weight of tradition – as in the refrain: 'No Change!' This old order is embodied in Gertrude, the inscrutable Countess of Groan, and Barquentine, her tyrannical Master of Ritual. It is challenged by three wayward children: Steerpike, the renegade kitchen

PHOTOGRAPH BY ALASTAIR MUIR

boy who seduces and murders his way up the social ladder; the Lady Fuchsia, destroyed by her forbidden love for him; and her brother, Lord Titus, the heir to Gormenghast who comes to embody the change that threatens its very existence. The voice of Gormenghast Castle manifests in a Chorus, a brooding physical presence against which these gifted children rebel.

My script provided the dramatic narrative for David's theatrical vision. During rehearsals he used theatre games and other 'play' situations to help the Ensemble explore these dark worlds of childhood. The actors took extraordinary risks to find their heightened characters: Hayley Carmichael's Fuchsia, Paul Hamilton's Flay and Di Sherlock's Gertrude are just three of the vivid portrayals that stay in my mind, even fifteen years on from the original production. As well as playing their individual characters, with some doubling up, the actors also worked together as the Chorus and as a true ensemble to realize David's remarkable theatrical coups.

Rather than trying to represent a naturalistic castle, David and the designer, Rae Smith, came up with a minimalist set: a raised platform above a backdrop of doors. All the other scenery was created by the Ensemble working with simple props: movable black screens, white poles and silks. Flay's journey to the underworld was realized with a choreographed shuffling of the screens, accompanied by the sounds of echoing footsteps and cracking knee-joints, dripping water

Above
The Twins

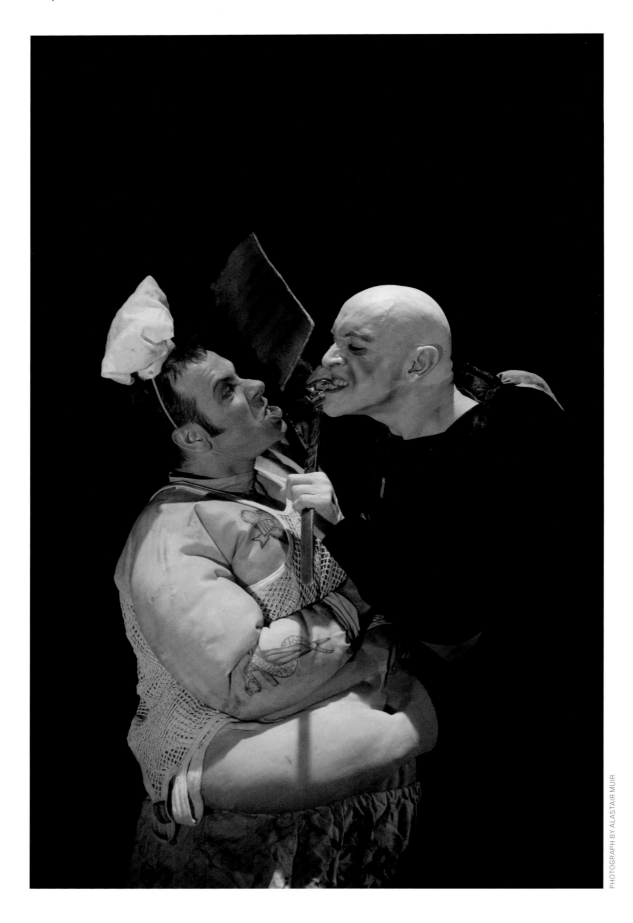

and crumbling masonry. The flood was powerfully suggested with a huge rippling white silk.

David Glass's imaginative direction, John Eacott's music and soundscapes, Rae Smith's design, Spike Mosley's lighting, Sally Owen's choreography and the physical versatility of the Ensemble – all these helped create the heightened, autonomous world of Gormenghast. David's greatest achievement was to weave these elements together to evoke a world that did justice to Peake's vision.

Although we had confidence in our stage version of Gormenghast, we were unprepared for the critical and popular acclaim the production received. It opened at the Alhambra Studio Theatre, Bradford, followed by a British tour which culminated at Battersea Arts Centre, London. The play subsequently transferred to the Lyric, Hammersmith, London, where it was brought back for a second run. Further national tours and three international British Council tours followed. It was gratifying that so many Mervyn Peake devotees felt our work was faithful to the spirit of the original and that even people who had not read the books were deeply affected by our dramatization.

Facing page
Flay and Swelter

Below
Titus and the Thing

PHOTOGRAPH BY ALASTAIR MUIR

Controlled Staging and Epic Emotion

DAVID GLASS

PHOTOGRAPH BY ALASTAIR MUIR

Above
The Thing

Facing page

Top left
The Countess and
Dr Prunesquallor

Top right
Fuchsia

Bottom
Steerpike and Fuchsia

In 1975, age sixteen, opening the Penguin edition of *Gormenghast* revealed a dark corridor leading directly to the adventure, terror and romance that is adolescence. My imagination was so engaged by Mervyn Peake's epic of ritualized oppression, it was as though my retinas had been tattooed with his world. His vision became mine. Such is the power of great imaginative literature on the young that it transforms our psychic DNA whilst giving us the illusion that this world has always existed within us and Peake had merely strapped on some strange Victorian viewing instrument straight out something from Prunesquallor's den, in order that we might see it.

Twenty years later I returned to the books, but this time I wondered whether we could transform the viewing device from literature into theatre. After carefully reading the books John Constable and I agreed that we must never show Gormenghast, never literalize the castle. Gormenghast must remain an enigmatic labyrinthine state of mind, not a place the audience should ever see.

In theatre we 'provoke, evoke and invoke'. The latter two became the principles of the Ensemble's approach to the books. The audience must leave the theatre sensing they had walked through the Groans' ancestral home when in fact they had merely peered into the velvet darkness of a fairly empty stage, filling what wasn't actually there with their imaginations. And anyway, as it happens, we only had enough dosh for eight actors and little or no set.

Unlike another fantasy epic I could mention Gormenghast has no magic spells, trolls or giants. The characters are driven by the great themes that have always enlivened theatre: Love, Greed and Death. This is the world of melodrama – and I don't mean that in the hammy pejorative sense. Melodrama is the theatre of powerful, expressive emotion. Emotion that appears to transform the scenic and musical qualities of the stage. It requires of the actors a physical commitment to the shapes, rhythms and internal intentions of their characters. Flay as embodied by Paul Hamilton or Julian Bleach was defined as much by his extraordinary shape

and walk on stage as he was by his unerring sense of loyalty to the House of Groan. When Titus (played by Pete Bailie) kills Steerpike (played by Rick Atlee) he thrusts the knife upwards, holding his dying enemy in a one-handed lift that astonishes the audience by its power and savagery, whilst also garnering Mr Bailie a fair amount of attention in the bar afterwards.

Another clue to the adaptation was found in Peake's Asian childhood. The stylized theatre of Chinese Opera and kabuki (which Peake may have seen) gave the designer Rae Smith and myself the ritualistic echo that sat at the heart of Titus's world. Titus is bound by ritual and, by drawing on elements of Asian theatre and combining this with melodrama, we hoped to create a tension between controlled staging and epic emotion.

All of this had to be driven by plot, character and conflict. John Constable lovingly served the books by recognizing that, although couched in grotesqueness, at their emotional heart is an epic coming-of-age story between Titus, Fuchsia and Steerpike. Looking at the moving drawings of Peake's children one can see his passionate, unsentimentalized belief in children and their resilience, brilliance and passion for living. John carefully walked the tightrope between filleting and finding the heart. Being a writer himself, John knew the respect due to Peake's original.

As I read the trilogy, over and over again, the indelible brilliant pictures that Peake creates pointed me to a visual and sounded spectacle. It was important to give the impression of an endlessly gloomy shrouded world, and yet every facial tick had to be registered in the cheap seats of the theatre, one hundred metres away. The answer was bright, sharply focused shafts of light into which the actors could move out of darkness and into Gothic intensity – aided of course by a dollop of smoke and vast amounts of dust. The sound and music of Gormenghast was perhaps the hardest element to discover. There is no sound in a book. The slow erosion of stone, scuttling of insects and snapping of Flay's knees became John Eacott's starting point. From this grew a simple descending chord structure which expressed the oppressive unending quality of the castle.

The energy of the books may appear at first ponderous; however, Peake counterpoints this with a playful, comic and lively energy that seems to defy the very stones of the castle he describes. To embrace this the ensemble of actors discovered an *élan* in the playing of the chorus and in each character.

For myself, reading the trilogy as a teenager, I felt Peake encouraging me to embrace the strange, the wonderful and the visionary. After bringing his work to the stage, this gift of thinking differently has inspired and informed all my subsequent work. It's very hard to remove tattoos from your eyes once they are there. Thank you, Mr Peake.

Above
Flay

Facing page

Top
Christopher Lee as Flay in the BBC production of *Gormenghast*

Below
Storyboard images from the BBC adaptation *Gormenghast*, continuing over pages 190–93

Wrestling with the Unfilmable

ESTELLE DANIEL

I spent five years talking about Gormenghast. The last five of the twentieth century. I followed people along corridors talking about it, round the eternal circle of BBC Television Centre. I droned on in air-conditioned offices in Los Angeles. I held forth on mobiles where I couldn't hear the answers on the other end; in castles and monasteries; on computers and in pen and ink. I shouted down the phone to Australia in the middle of my night, and I harangued polite foreign TV executives who didn't understand me or Gormenghast (and never would) on the Croisette in Cannes.

I wrote many thousands of words about Gormenghast – a volume for Lord Groan's library or a box of documents for Barquentine. Such is the richness of the material provided by Peake that there always seems to be more to say.

First, a fragmented timeline of landmarks in the making of a Gormenghast adaptation. The 1980s: A team headed by Michael Wearing at the BBC (including me) start remaking classics such as *Pride and Prejudice* for a modern audience. Meanwhile somewhere in Hollywood, *Gormenghast* is not being made – Sting, Terry Gilliam and sundry producers (who held the film rights over the years) can explain why elsewhere. The 1990s: Computer-generated images are becoming affordable on TV budgets (just). *Gormenghast* is commissioned for the millennium as an extension of the modern classic serial. 1996: I take over as producer and Michael Wearing asks me a single question 'Where is Gormenghast?' 1997: I visit a Tibetan-style monastery in Ladakh and think I may have answered that question, as the visual quest for Gormenghast starts to reverberate with the East. Back in London research on Peake's life reveals that he grew up in China. Sometime later we show Mark Thompson, now BBC Director General, Christopher Hobbs's new Eastern-influenced designs and director Andy Wilson's irresistible cartoon-style storyboards. 'James Cameron on a BBC budget,' says Thompson. 17 November 1998: Thirtieth anniversary of the death of Mervyn Peake. BBC greenlights the films. 9 July 1999: Mervyn Peake's birthday; we finish filming. 17 January 2000: Gormenghast is screened on the BBC.

GORMENGHAST
OPENING SEQUENCE (AFTER TITLES).

IMAGE OF CASTLE REFLECTED IN IRIS OF MR. CHALK'S EYE

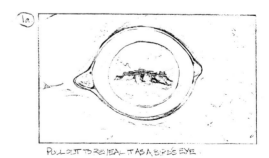

PULL OUT TO REVEAL IT AS A BIRD'S EYE.

PULL OUT FURTHER TO SEE MR. CHALK FLYING.

PULL BACK FURTHER & BEHIND MR. CHALK TO REVEAL
HE'S FLYING ABOVE CASTLE.

MOVE IN BEHIND HIM AS HE FLIES TOWARD CASTLE LANDSCAPE.

MR. CHALK CRUISES PAST STONEWORK.

V. LOW ANGLE. MR. CHALK CRUISES THROUGH GAP IN WALLS.

BEHIND MR CHALK TOWARDS GERTRUDE'S TOWER
THROUGH CANYON OF BUILDINGS. OTHER BIRDS CIRCLE TOWER.

Film-making is an intensely practical medium. Unless you can see how to do something you might as well not proceed. So without certain key elements falling into place – both creative and physical – we couldn't have done it. Here are one or two of the important things. Contemporary resonance: the turn of the century, Tony Blair's New Labour, Tories in meltdown under William Hague (there were political columns in the newspapers comparing this to Gormenghast), distressed Royals warring internally and struggling to retain a united front. The timing was somehow right.

Then there was the wealth of visual and research material that emerged, feeding into the production. It seemed to endlessly multiply – character drawings by Peake, set designs for a Gormenghast opera, letters from Graham Greene, Dylan Thomas, Orson Welles and other great writers and artists of the twentieth century, illuminating Peake's world from hidden angles. It felt like privileged film-making of the most extraordinary kind.

Finding Steerpike was pivotal. Peter Paterson wrote in the *Daily Mail*: 'The greatest discovery and the undoubted star of *Gormenghast* was Jonathan Rhys Meyers as Steerpike. This was a performance that mixed villainy and charm, violence and gentleness in one awesome, swashbuckling package. When he's big in Hollywood we'll remember that it was in the wonderful *Gormenghast* that he made his name.' I thought of this the other day, watching Jonathan Rhys Meyers having sex with Scarlett Johannson in a cornfield, in Woody Allen's *Match Point*.

As we moved into production with *Gormenghast* there was the hint of an appetite for fantasy on the TV screens. The BBC had not touched it since *Dr Who*. It is easy to forget now how impossible it all seemed without computer-generated images. It might now appear that this *Gormenghast* was, in typical Peake style, a little out of sync, ahead of its time, providing a small-screen taste of what was to come with the Tolkien, Potter and Narnia adaptations.

Here are a few facts about the *Gormenghast* films. Over the series an average of 4.5 million viewers watched every week. It had an impressively young audience profile. A total of 22,500 people had bought the tie-in by the time it was half broadcast, twice as many as the publisher expected. People ring BBC phone-ins all the time saying that their children won't sit and watch *Pride and Prejudice*, nor will they read the books. One of my thoughts was to make a classic serial that a younger audience would watch and which would motivate them to go away and read the book. Maybe this epic story with its six murders, two seductions and three tragic deaths might do the trick. 'A plot', as London's *Evening Standard* wrote when the books were published, 'which makes Richard III's seem cautious, uncomplicated, unimaginative and unduly sentimental'. So these figures gave me more pleasure than almost anything else.

There was a long list of Royal Television Society (RTS) and British Academy of Film and Television Arts (BAFTA) nominations and awards across the various categories. The press cuttings for *Gormenghast* fill four albums – and that does not include the foreign press. The bulk of the writing was lavish in its praise and makes for satisfying reading. Where it was not complimentary, it was passionate and promoted lively debate. The London press 'swooned for *Gormenghast*', reported the *New York Post*. Consider the following:

> The creation of *Gormenghast* takes matters into another dimension . . . It is an indication of the power of this amazing dramatization that much of Peake's preoccupation, with what might and might not be mad, streams off the screen. Some may find this unsettling, but then many of us find Grimm's fairytales and *King Lear* unsettling, too. *Gormenghast* occupies a parallel universe close to them. Watch it.
>
> (Christopher Dunkley, *Financial Times*)

Or these:

> The new BBC adaptation of the Gormenghast novels wrestles with the unfilmable – and comes out on top.
>
> (*Independent*, 21 January 2000)

> Everything about *Gormenghast* is bigger, wilder, and more allusive than television is designed to contain . . . After the initial shock, we buy into this world for two reasons. First, because it is screamingly funny; second, because it turns out not to be as outlandish as it seems. This is not an epic; it is too intimate . . . the BBC has wrestled this supposedly intractable masterpiece to the ground in grand style.'
>
> (Andrew Billen, *New Statesman*, 24 January 2000)

The Times called the films 'landmark television with knobs on'. Then there were some particularly engaging pieces in the press in the United States, where the book was less well-known. *Time* magazine wrote:

> This lavish mini-series follows Steerpike (Jonathan Rhys Meyers), a charismatic kitchen boy who insinuates and murders his way to power within the tired, decaying House of Groan. Unlike many American fantasy minis, it's neither a ponderous classics lesson nor a sugar-coated trifle, but a grotesquely funny, vulgar and penetrating tale of class and demagogy.

More significantly *Gormenghast* entered the *Zeitgeist*, with phrases such as 'Steerpike, the Mandelsonian kitchen boy' scattered through the daily papers. Political columnists and assorted hacks used 'Gormenghastian' as an adjective to describe various British institutions – including the press and the BBC. *Gormenghast* also appeared on ITV in an episode of *Home and Away*, as a must-read book for one of the characters. An intriguing public debate started up, trying to pin the work down, just as it had done when the books were first published. There were even those (predictably on Radio 4) who tried to argue that television drama should

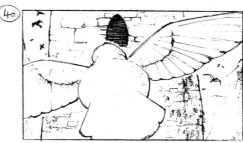

MOVE UP BEYOND HIM AS HE APPROACHES A WINDOW.

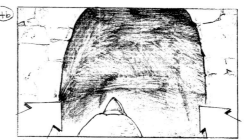

PUSH IN AND BECOME MR. CHALK'S P.O.V. AS HE ENTERS WINDOW.

PUSH THROUGH WINDOW.

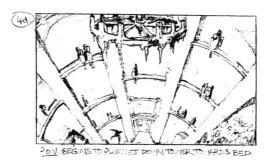

P.O.V. BEGINS TO PLUMMET DOWN TOWER TOWARDS BED.

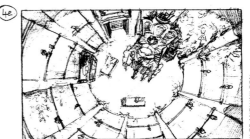

CONTINUE PLUMMETTING DOWN TOWARDS BED
SEE PRUNESQUALOR, 4 NURSES & GERTRUDE ON BED.
OTHER BIRDS CIRCLE.

RUSHING DOWN TOWARDS BED AS IF CAMERA WILL HIT IT.
GERTRUDE IS IN CHILDBIRTH.

CAMERA SWOOPS IN OVER GERTRUDE.

CAMERA SWOOPS OVER GERTRUDE'S FACE AS SHE CRIES OUT.

CUT TO: MR. CHALK ALIGHTS ON HEADBOARD.

CUT TO: OVER GERTRUDE'S HEAD.
PRUNESQUALLOR: "I SEE GENETALIA. IT'S OF A SEX, YOUR LADYSHIP."

be grounded in history and social realism. The audience – in particular students and twenty-somethings – wrote in large numbers to the papers and the BBC in response. The strength of feeling was striking. I was reminded of the letter from C. S. Lewis to Peake. 'People now all seem to want a "slice of life" . . . or a "comment on life",' he wrote. 'To me those who merely comment on experience seem far less valuable than those who add to it, who make me experience what I never experienced before. I would not for anything have missed *Gormenghast*. It has the hallmark of a true myth: i.e. you have seen nothing like it before you read the work, but after that you see things like it everywhere.'

The work of Peake's unique imagination seems to unfailingly penetrate the subconscious and stir up an atmosphere of strongly felt debate and conflicting emotions. Perhaps this is simply an inevitable consequence of his examination of the deepest and darkest regions of human experience. Before he died, Mervyn Peake wrote some notes towards a fourth volume called *Titus Awakes*. At the end of *Titus Alone*, Titus has been inexorably drawn back to Gormenghast. But he decides not to return to the castle. He turns away and goes down the mountain, where he spends the night in a barn. He has a nightmare and in this dream he sees Flay, the ancestral butler, and Swelter, cook to the Groan household, once more. It was of course the dispute between Flay and Swelter and what lies behind it that unleashed the evil kitchen boy on Gormenghast and triggered the destruction that followed. I have always thought this clash is somewhere close to the heart of things.

This is what Titus sees in his dream: 'For a moment they beamed at one another, this dire couple in a mixture of sweat and leather – and then their mutual hatred settled in again, like a foul plant or fungi. And yet they held hands, and as they moved across the arena of Titus' brain they sang to one another. Swelter in a thin fluted voice, and Flay reminiscent of a rusty key turning in a lock. They sang of joy, with murder in their eyes. They sang of love, with bile upon their tongues.' I have given some thought to how to film this little scene. It satisfies me as a partial answer, left by Mervyn Peake, to the conflict of emotions question. It would be fun to add it on to the DVD as an extra scene, meant as a visual reply for fans as well as critics of all flavours, Radio 4 presenters, the ghost of Kingsley Amis and the whole merry band. Until I work out how to do it, I will content myself with waiting for the next *Gormenghast*. Producers may come, and producers may go, as Barquentine might have said, but Gormenghast remains.

CUT TO: OVER GERTRUDE'S HEAD.
PRUNESQUALLOR: "I SEE GENETALIA. IT'S OF A SEX, YOUR LADYSHIP."

C/U GERTRUDE: "WHAT KIND?"
+ CONTINUE ON THIS C/U.

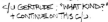

C/U PRUNESQUALLOR: "A FINE SEX. A BRAND NEW GROAN, ETC."
+ CONTINUE ON THIS C/U.

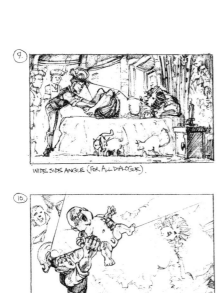

9.

WIDE SIDE ANGLE (FOR ALL DIALOGUE).

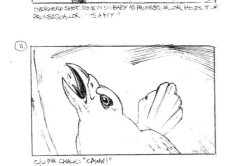

10.

OVERHEAD SHOT. MOVE IN ON BABY AS PRUNESQUALLOR HOLDS IT UP.
PRUNESQUALLOR: "IT'S A BOY."

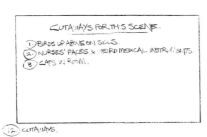

11.

C/U MR. CHALK: "CAWW!"

CUTAWAYS FOR THIS SCENE.

1) BIRDS UP ABOVE ON SILLS.
2) NURSES' FACES & WEIRD MEDICAL INSTRUMENTS.
3) CATS IN ROOM.

12. CUTAWAYS.

SCENE 3.

13. PULL OUT FROM KEYHOLE TO SEE OLD RETAINER'S FACE.
PRUNESQUALLORS V/O: "IT'S A BOY!"

13. PULL OUT TO RETAINER STANDS. MADE PUSH PAST HIM INTO ROOM.

13b. PUSH IN AS RETAINER MOVES FORWARD & TURNS. "A BOY."
REVEAL HUGE, DANK CORRIDOR WITH FIGURE AT END.

SCENE 3A - ADDITIONAL TO SCRIPT.

14.

2ND RETAINER AT END OF CORRIDOR HEARS, TURNS & GOES TO WINDOW.

15.

RETAINER SHOUTS OUT OF WINDOW WITH CGI VIEW OF GORMENGHAST.
RETAINER: "IT'S A BOY!"

SCENE 4

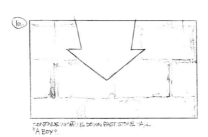

1.

ECHO V/O: "A BOY"
WHIPPING DOWN PAST STONE WALL.

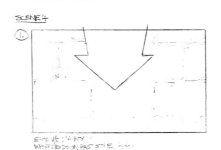

1a.

CONTINUE WHIPPING DOWN PAST STONE WALL.
"A BOY".

1b.

ON A DISSOLVE ARE FEET SOLDIER TURNS TO STAND. IN BEHIND HIM.

1c.

WHOOSH OVER HIS SHOULDER & DOWN STEPS.

1d.

WHOOSH DOWN STEPS & TOWARDS A STONE DOORWAY.

SCENE 5.

1.

CUT TO OTHER SIDE OF STONE DOORWAY & CONTINUE MOVE
PAST WASHERWOMEN.

1a.

CONTINUE MOVE PAST REAL STONE TROUGH. WASHERWOMEN
THROW CLOTHES INTO AIR. "A BOY! A SON FOR GROAN!"

SCENE 6.

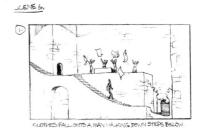

1.

CLOTHES FALL ONTO A MAN WALKING DOWN STEPS BELOW.

2.

C/U FLAY OBSCURED BY A PIECE OF CLOTHING.
V/O: "A BOY! A SON! A NEW EARL! A NEW GROAN!"

11 The Last Years

G. PETER WINNINGTON

To north, south, east or west, turning at will, it was not long before his landmarks fled him. Gone was the outline of his mountainous home. Gone that torn world of towers. Gone the grey lichen; gone the black ivy. Gone was the labyrinth that fed his dreams. Gone ritual, his marrow and his bane. Gone boyhood. Gone.

From *Titus Alone*

In the spring of 1955, Peake was invited to join a varied group of writers who were planning a television documentary on contemporary Yugoslavia. It was his first trip abroad since his visit to the Continent at the end of the war, and he enjoyed depicting the unfamiliar sights. In the end, though, the projected programme was never made and Peake's paintings and drawings remained largely unseen.

About this time Peake's health began to decline. The first symptom he noticed was a shaking hand, which hampered his drawing, and then the shaking spread to his arms and legs. Thinking that it was caused by overwork – for in addition to his teaching, painting and drawing he was investing much time in writing his plays – a kind friend (who insisted on anonymity) paid for him and Maeve to take a holiday in Spain. Again he sketched avidly, and thanks to a personal introduction they were able to see some of Spain's great paintings inside the Prado, which was actually closed to the public at that point. It was a good holiday but could not cure Peake's condition.

He was suffering from the first stages of Parkinson's disease. On the basis of biographical evidence, a Canadian neurologist, Demetrios J. Sahlas, has identified the particular variety that affected Peake as Dementia with Lewy Bodies (DLB), which is commensurate with the delusions, hallucinations and impaired visuospatial function that he came to experience. The disease also reduced his attention span, making it impossible for him to concentrate on writing or drawing for more than a few minutes at a time. The effect of this can be seen in the many short chapters of *Titus Alone*, which he had great difficulty in finishing. By 1959, when the book was with Eyre and Spottiswoode, he was unable to respond to their request for revisions, and with a heavy heart Maeve agreed to their suggestions on his behalf. The result was not satisfactory. Ten years later, Langdon Jones revised it for a second edition.

Facing page and above
Elderly men sketched in
Dubrovnik, 1955

Top and bottom left, and above

Sketches in pen and wash of men
in Yugoslavia, 1955

Bottom right
A fishwife in Dubrovnik

Drawings made in and around
Madrid, Easter 1956

Re-editing *Titus Alone*

LANGDON JONES

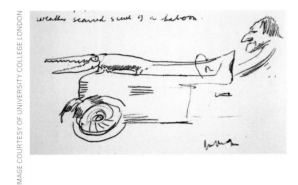

weather scarred skull of a baboon

Above
Muzzlehatch and his car, with the
crocodile skull on its bonnet, from
the manuscript of *Titus Alone*

Facing page
Sketch from the manuscript of
Titus Alone

It was during the early 1960s that I first heard of Mervyn Peake, largely thanks to Michael Moorcock, who urged me to try the Titus books. Of course, people being contrary creatures, pressures like that tend to have the opposite effect. So it was some years before I first read the monumental opening sentence of *Titus Groan* and became drawn into a wonderful, alien, extravagant, funny and eccentric world, emerging three books later to find that I had been changed and enriched by my visit to Gormenghast.

I knew that *Titus Alone* had been written at a time when Peake was fighting the illness that ultimately consumed him, so I was not surprised to find it a slightly less polished story than the other two. There were quite a lot of anomalous passages, repetitions, non-sequiturs and so on, and I put them down to Peake's struggle to finish the book while he could. However, although the execution was somewhat flawed, the burden of the book was more weighty and more relevant than that of the other two volumes. While they told a human story of corruption, ambition and social stasis – something that could attract us without involving us except as empathetic observers – the last book dealt with altogether deeper matters that had come to the surface in a horribly spectacular way in the revelations of the Holocaust, the fire-bombing of Dresden and the detonation of two atomic bombs. These were things that showed what people like us were capable of and made us examine ourselves more closely and more uneasily.

At this time I was involved with Mike Moorcock's magazine *New Worlds*, for which I reviewed *A Reverie of Bone*, looking at the poems in the context of Peake's other work. Peake was then virtually unknown in the literary world; indeed, after the review came out I received a letter from a London publisher who assumed that it must be a work of fiction and Peake himself an imaginary Borgesian character. I found it astonishing that an artist of such enormous talent and diversity should not be recognized.

Shortly afterwards I unexpectedly received a letter from Mervyn's wife Maeve,

thanking me for the review and telling me that she had taken it to the home where Peake was then resident and had read it to him. She told me 'he had got something good from it'.

Subsequently Mike took me to meet Maeve. She turned out to be a slender, poised and graceful woman with a gaze that could be piercing. I found her to be a curious mixture of characteristics. She was wonderfully warm and generous but at the same time had a strangely withdrawn demeanour about her, as though she were receiving messages from some distant star. As one got to know her better one felt that despite her intelligence she found certain things in life to be puzzling, and recorded them without fully understanding them, ready to add to the report she was ultimately going to send home. I think, without wishing to sound maudlin, that in fact she had a purity of soul, which made certain aspects of life seem strange to her. She had a total respect for all forms of art, and one sensed that she felt there was nothing in this life more important, a viewpoint that can only be respected. She told me that American film producers had been interested in the Titus books, but she was prepared to let them be used only if she could have the ultimate decision as to what ended up on the screen. This is one of the reasons why we have never, to date, seen a film of the trilogy.

She put me at ease from the start, and the more I got to know Maeve the more I liked her. I loved the way she assumed her own perceptions were general. I seem to remember her saying that sometimes, of course, we were inhibited from eating some fruit, like peaches, because of its resemblance to parts of the human anatomy. She looked at things from this slightly unusual angle, but it was a view that could be enlightening. I remember her saying that a writer I greatly admired at the time had been to visit. I eagerly asked her what he was like. The puzzled expression appeared in her eyes, momentarily. 'He's a very *emotional* man,' she said. She told me, and to this day I don't know whether she was serious, that Mervyn had mentioned that one of the formative influences on the Titus books was the rules of cricket. She

IMAGE COURTESY OF HENRY BOXER GALLERY

Left
Pencil sketch of helmeted figure

Right
'Titus leaving Gormenghast'

Facing page
Nude model at the Central School
of Art

spoke about Mervyn and his work a great deal, and I regret that my leaky memory does not retain more of what she said.

In terms of their sexual content, some of my stories and poems in *New Worlds* pushed some of the boundaries of the time. She always told me when she read something of mine, and that she found it – interesting. Her refined sensibilities could lead to misunderstanding, as I discovered when I worked on *Titus Alone*. 'Words can be a series of facts,' said Muzzlehatch in the first draft. Maeve had typed out the draft from handwritten sheets, and 'facts' was her interpretation of what she saw. This word had been crossed through by Peake and corrected. In the next version Muzzlehatch spoke more enigmatically, saying that 'Words can be a series of forts.' From the original draft it was clear that he been talking of something far more vaporous than stone.

I discovered that *Titus Alone* had been very heavily edited by the publisher and that Maeve shared Peake's distress at the changes. He was, however, too ill by then to be able to do anything about them. He was aware of his deterioration and knew that he had only a limited time to work on the book. One can imagine the frustration of trying to create with blunted tools and then realizing that his creation had been additionally sculpted by others. Maeve brought the original manuscripts to me, and I spent a magical afternoon going through them, reading new material and knowing that I was one of a mere handful of people who had seen it. As I did so, I saw how great the changes had been. Maeve allowed me to proceed with the restoration, and in retrospect I am amazed and gratified at the level of trust this implied.

Nowadays some people feel very indignant about what was originally done to the book. And it is true that the editors did go a little overboard. But things are different now. The books have a pedigree, and a history. People now know about Peake's illness. In those days the editors were confronted by a chaotic typescript,

written by a difficult author whose star had apparently set, and were conscious that they had to turn it into a commercial novel. They did so by carrying out major surgery, not all of which was entirely successful.

I saw there was a lot that had gone. I also saw that the editors had a frame of reference which put Gormenghast firmly in the Middle Ages. The science-fiction aspects, indeed, the twentieth-century aspects of *Titus Alone*, were very difficult for them to swallow. They could not remove these altogether, simply because they were an integral part of the book. Instead of leaving them alone they took the worst possible course, of changing some of them. Possibly the most egregious example of this was the one I quoted in my introduction to my edition of the book. The original edition read:

> 'You must take me there. At once,' said Cheeta, recoiling inwardly, for his age was palpable.
> 'Why should I?' he said.
> 'You will be paid . . . well paid. We will fly.'
> 'What's that?' said the septuagenarian.

Peake originally wrote:

> 'You will be paid . . . well paid. We will go by helicopter.'
> 'What's that?' said the septuagenarian.

There was a striking moment when a baby annihilates an ant colony with a stream of urine, and for a moment we assume the viewpoint of the ants. The fact

Above
Models at the Central School
of Art

that this was virtually repeated a few pages further on I took as evidence of Peake's deterioration. I discovered, though, that Peake had been aware of the repetition and had deleted its second occurrence. The editors restored the paragraph.

I felt that the time was right for an edition of the book that would be as close as possible to what Peake had originally written, warts and all. It seemed that, indeed, it might prove to be less verrucose than the book as published.

There were a number of scripts of the book, the most interesting of which was the handwritten first draft, complete with little margin sketches. This draft had been typed out, and additional changes made, and a further typescript prepared prior to submission. The difficulty of the project was to incorporate the changes Peake had subsequently made, while ignoring those that had been made on the instructions of the editors.

Maeve very kindly let me take the typescripts and drafts home with me, where I was able to work on the book at my own pace. At the beginning, though, there were occasions when I worked on it with Maeve. It was difficult to read Peake's handwriting, in an ink that was brownish in hue, but in time I was to become fluent.

Above
Owl-like bird in wash, 1956

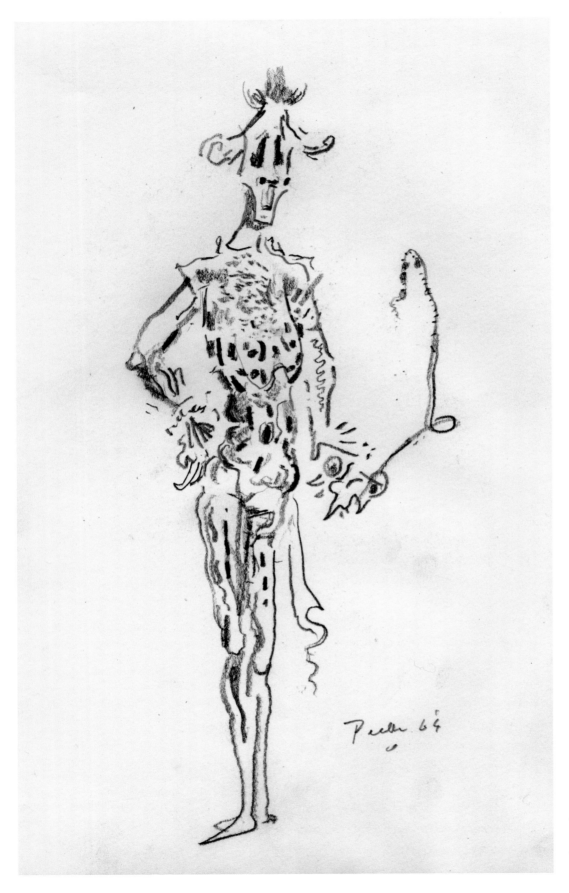

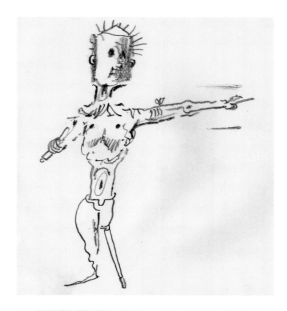

I remember one happy afternoon when Maeve dictated to me a whole new section of the book, the party at Lady Cusp-Canine's – snatches of overheard party conversation, some of which were quite surreal – when at times we laughed so much she was incapable of reading aloud, and I was unable to type.

As the book began to take shape it became clear that in the new version the latter part of the story, dealing with the scientist, that embodiment of evil, and his seductive daughter Cheeta, was to be much more important. Peake had been profoundly affected by the suffering he had witnessed when he entered Germany at the

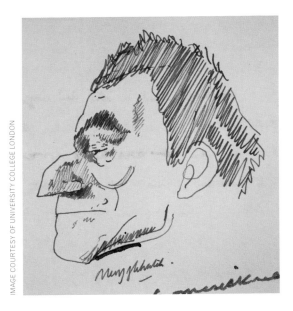

end of the war. And in the recursive vision of the artist, he was affected, too, by his reaction to it.

Much of the book contains imagery that could have come from the war. The Under-River, with its assorted crowd of beggars, tinkers, philosophers-manqués and mendicants, was perhaps not so far removed from the sewers of Warsaw where many of the ill-fated Jews hid from the invaders. The factory with the faces at the windows was a reflection of something Peake observed in real life while in Germany, an image that he found very affecting. Veil and the Black Rose portrayed the inhuman nature of those who willingly give themselves up to evil and the hopeless acquiescence of those who are its victims. And Titus's reaction to the Black Rose and to Muzzlehatch's suffering, his compassion together with its undercurrent – the weary repulsion he feels – echo some of the feelings of Peake when he observed the victims of Belsen.

Reconstructing the book was a largely mechanical exercise. There were a few places where I would have preferred to consult Peake about changes but obviously could not do so. One of these changes, and one that still causes me pain, was the deletion of parts of Titus's delirium, which I carried out on the depressingly mundane grounds that in it he spoke of characters he had not yet met, although the reader was already familiar with them.

Here, for the sake of completeness, is that section as it originally appeared:

The castle is a-float. Steerpike, my enemy, swims under water, a dagger between his teeth. Yet I killed him. I killed him dead.

Come here and you may see old Slingshott's face . . . Slingshott of the mines with salt in his mouth. We will dance together on the battlements. The turrets are white with bird-lime. It is like phosphorus. Join hands with me, Slingshott and Muzzlehatch and Juno, loveliest of all, and step out into space. We will not fall alone for as we pass window after window, a score of heads will bob along beside us, grinning like ten-to-three. Crack-bell and Sober-Carter: Veil and the Black Rose: Jonah and the squirrel: Cusp-Canine and the Grasses . . .

Towards the end of the book the writing is curious. Peake's gift of finding precisely the right word to turn a description from something mundane into something profound did not desert him. The only thing that betrayed the fact that there was something desperately wrong was a certain loosening of control that became apparent in the latter part of the book. This part deals with the mad scientist responsible for the darts and globes that constantly observe, like mobile CCTV cameras, and also the rays that destroy Muzzlehatch's zoo. The book does not express an anti-technology point of view, but it does recognize the damage that technology, used irresponsibly, can wreak. Titus encounters the scientist just before Muzzlehatch's bomb goes off, like the atomic bombs that were dropped on Japan.

Above
Study of Muzzlehatch, from the manuscript of *Titus Alone*

Facing page
Sitting bird, late 1950s

IMAGE COURTESY OF CHRIS BEETLES GALLERY

IMAGE COURTESY OF CHRIS BEETLES GALLERY

Above left
Negress, 1951

Above right
Study of a girl in pencil, c.1955

Above
Maeve Gilmore and Mervyn Peake
in Wallington 1956

Facing page
Illustrations for Peake's own
Rhyme of the Flying Bomb

Even as he spoke a light appeared in the sky in the direction of the sound.

'That would be the death of many men,' said Muzzlehatch. 'That would be the last roar of the golden fauna: the red of the world's blood: doom is one step closer. It was the fuse that did it. The blue fuse. My dear man,' he said, turning to Anchor, 'only look at the sky.'

Sure enough it was taking on a life of its own. Unhealthy as a neglected sore, skeins of transparent fabric wavered across the night sky, peeling off, one after another to reveal yet fouler tissues in a fouler empyrean.

The figure of the mad scientist was subsequently to become rather overused, although at the time when the book was written it was perhaps not quite the cliché it is today, and Peake's version undergoes an interesting transformation once he loses his power, becoming a grotesque child. Pretty consistently, Peake referred to him as 'the death-ray scientist'. I decided to remove the adjective as I felt that, taken in conjunction with the slight relaxing of control in the writing, it might affect the status of the book with the critics, and at that time Peake's reputation was not as solid as it is today. It was a change I felt didn't need justification, but, as it has been criticized by one writer, perhaps an explanation is necessary. As I said in the introduction to the revised edition, there were places where, had the author been able to judge, I would have conferred with him.

Many aspects of the book reflect what was happening to its author and for this reason are difficult to read, even today. A particularly poignant moment comes when Muzzlehatch says, 'There must be something wrong with my brain.' But despite the fact that Peake was holding the book together by sheer force of will, it still possesses considerable visionary power. In his ultimate rejection of his home Titus expresses the profound loss that was being experienced by his author.

However, the resolution of the book shows that even then Peake's natural optimism did not desert him. Passing from the world of *Titus Alone* Titus may leave wreckage in his wake, but, overall, it is a rather better place than when he entered it. There is perhaps less humour to be found in the last book, but even so the reader does not arrive at the conclusion of the story weighed down with a surfeit of horror. Perhaps the open ending of *Titus Alone* is appropriate, because we finish the three books having been given a glimpse – lasting at least two decades – of Titus's world and we sense that his adventures, and the life of Gormenghast, will continue without us, proceeding in a direction we cannot guess at.

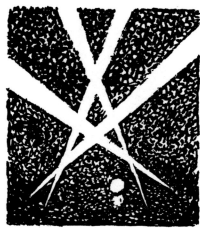

When the reconstruction was complete Maeve submitted it to the publishers, who were clearly unhappy as it implicitly criticized their editorial policies. Eventually they succumbed after pressure from others, but even so made alterations to my introduction in such a way as to make the amount of new material in the book appear less than it was.

The trilogy stands as a monument to a wonderful, romantic, visionary talent, as does the whole of Peake's *œuvre*. It is only on those occasions when one is able to view all aspects of Peake's work, as in some of the comprehensive exhibitions that have been mounted, that one can appreciate on a visceral level how wide-ranging his powers were. We are living in a society where the visual is gaining in importance, while the verbal is becoming seemingly more superfluous, a world of wonderful visuals allied with malformed text. Much of Peake's work is visual; it is a world of which he is the master, in his drawings and his paintings but also in the visual aspects of his poems and novels. But Peake's genius extends to the verbal, where his style is conservative, precise, poetic and colourful. The twentieth century might come to be seen as perhaps the last time when the word was supreme, and it is appropriate that this great verbal utterance was made when it was. One thing is certain: artists like Peake, who are capable of excelling in so many different fields and to such an extent are rare elements in this universe of ours.

I, for one, will remain always grateful for the opportunity I was given to come into contact with his work, his life, and indeed his family.

Valediction

Above
The frontispiece from Mervyn Peake's commission in 1960 from the Folio Society to illustrate Honoré de Balzac's *Droll Stories*, thought to be the last illustration he produced

The last ten years of Peake's life were increasing difficult for him and his family. His attention span being short, Maeve had to read time and again the stories by Balzac that he illustrated for the Folio Society. As for the illustrations that Dent wanted for *The Rhyme of the Flying Bomb*, they were produced under most adverse conditions, for the pen itself would fall from his hand and Maeve had to retrieve it. Thereafter, Peake's drawing skill was present only sporadically. Suddenly the shaking would stop for a few minutes, and he would sketch. But for the most part he depended on his wife for everything.

There was no treatment for Parkinson's disease in those days, and the remedies that were attempted, electric shock treatment and later a brain operation, were ineffective and possibly destructive. Although Maeve dedicated her days to looking after her husband, the time came when he had to be institutionalized. She crossed London twice a week, bringing him paper, pens and pencils, some sweets and her love, but most of the time he was far away. He died, in her brother's home for the terminally ill, on 17 November 1968, just as his reputation was starting to revive, thanks to the publication of the Titus books as Penguin Modern Classics.

Five years later, the anarchist Arthur Moyse, artist and art critic, cartoonist and London bus conductor, wrote of his brief encounter with Peake:

It was at the private opening of a restaurant, and I found myself seated opposite an artist whom I had recently abused in print, and he abused me and his mistress without favouring either. Then I realized that sitting next to me was Mervyn Peake and his lovely wife. I have always admired his work as an artist, and I was honoured and excited to be in his company. His illness was in an advanced stage, and I sat there in awe and admired the attention his wife showed him. We ate the Spanish food and drank the wine, yet always and to this day I was aware of the presence of Mervyn Peake, crippled in body but with soft shining eyes bright with intelligence watching me and listening to the conversation.

I don't think he made any coherent statements, but I know he tried to speak and I watched his wife bending her head to listen to him and she aided him.

We remember a certain boy at school, a soldier in the army, a brief moment with some woman in some forgotten town, and they become fixed in our mind and in our memory for a moment of pleasure, of fear or of happiness. That evening with the guitars playing, the candles dying one by one, the quarrelling artist and his model, is part of my life memory because I sat with Mervyn Peake and broke bread with him.

Above
A late painting of a cat

Above
The Curé of Azay le Rideau, *Droll Stories*

Top right
A courtier's false wife, *Droll Stories*

Bottom right
The first frontispiece produced for *Droll Stories* which was submitted but rejected

Sources

IMAGE COURTESY OF CHRIS BEETLES GALLERY

Unless otherwise indicated, the place of publication is London. The publisher and date of Peake's works are given in the select bibliography below.

Page

6   'If I could see' from *Shapes and Sounds*, p. 17

13 Introduction revised from an essay first published in the *Sunday Telegraph*, 16 January 2000

13 'He has magic in his pen' from a review of *Titus Groan* by Charles Morgan in the *Sunday Times*, 31 March 1946, p. 3

13 'the most fashionable in England' from *The Naked Civil Servant* (Cape, 1968) p. 141

13 'aggressively three-dimensional' from Anthony Burgess's introduction to the second edition of *Titus Groan* (1968)

13 'unique, dark and majestic' from *A World Away* (Gollancz, 1970), p. 19

15 'If we went out' from *A World Away* (Gollancz, 1970), p. 142

15 'a bad fantasy writer' in *New Maps of Hell: A Survey of Science Fiction* (New York: Harcourt Brace Jovanovich, 1960), p. 153

15 'the smashing of another window pane' from Peake's introduction to his *Drawings*, p. 9

15 'It's not so much their blindness', ibid.

16 'After all, there are no rules' from Peake's introduction to his *Drawings*, p. 11

19 'To live at all' from *The Glassblowers*, p. 3

19 'Art is ultimately sorcery' from Peake's introduction to his *Drawings*, p. 8

21 'old plank': all Dr Peake's words are taken from his unpublished *Memoirs of a Doctor in China* (1948)

25 'as though they had been flown over from Croydon' from Peake's 'Notes for a Projected Autobiography' printed in *Peake's Progress*, pp. 471–5

26 'Mervyn was always very kind' from 'The Crested Wave' in *Mervyn Peake Review*, Vol. 11 (Autumn 1980), p. 7

28 'in narrowing perspective' from *Titus Groan* (2nd edition), p. 19

31 'One is clumsy at first' from *The Craft of the Lead Pencil*

31 'My first memory of Mervyn' from 'The Crested Wave' in *Mervyn Peake Review*, Vol. 11 (Autumn 1980), p. 8

31 'quite brilliant in both perception and vitality' and 'You may be turning out one of our greatest future Old Boys' from *Mervyn Peake* by John Watney (Michael Joseph, 1976), pp. 36 and 35 respectively

36 'walked up the Champs Elysées' from *Mervyn Peake: A Personal Memoir* by Gordon Smith (Gollancz, 1984), pp. 15–16

41 'His way of teaching' from 'Mervyn Peake at the Westminster Art School 1936–39' by Diana Gardner, *Mervyn Peake Review*, Vol. 10 (Spring 1980), p. 18

41 'He took me to the Tate' from 'The Crested Wave' in *Mervyn Peake Review*, Vol. 11 (Autumn 1980), p. 8

41 'attracted a good deal of notice' from 'Mervyn Peake at the Westminster Art School 1936–39' by Diana Gardner, *Mervyn Peake Review*, Vol. 10 (Spring 1980), p. 18

49 'For Maeve' from *The Glassblowers*, p. 30

49 'Out of my appalling shyness' from *A World Away* (Gollancz, 1970), p. 13

49   'almost in passing' from 'Mervyn Peake at the Westminster Art School 1936–39' by Diana Gardner, *Mervyn Peake Review*, Vol. 10 (Spring 1980), p. 20

50   'To Maeve' is the dedication poem in *Shapes and Sounds*

51   'Grottoed beneath your ribs' from *The Glassblowers*, p. 4

65   'The Army would be glad' from a letter to the secretary of the War Artists' Advisory Committee dated 17 April 1941, printed in *Peake Studies*, Vol. 2, No. ii (Summer 1991), p. 7

65   'Granted, I'm hopeless' from *Mervyn Peake: A Personal Memoir* by Gordon Smith (Gollancz, 1984), p. 82

75   'The Consumptive' from *The Glassblowers*, p. 15

77   'Victims' from *A Reverie of Bone*, p. 7

79   'I predict for Titus' from *Tatler & Bystander*, 3 April 1946, pp. 23 and 28

93   John Wood's contribution is excerpted from 'Mervyn Peake: A Pupil Remembers', *Mervyn Peake Review*, Vol. 12 (Spring 1981), pp. 15–28

103 'a prince who with a line of kings for lineage' from Peake's introduction to his *Drawings*, p. 8

104 'a sort of flagseller's night out' in *Punch*, 28 February 1945

104 'the publishers thought that it would be unfair' from "Mervyn Peake: A Pupil Remembers' by John Wood, *Mervyn Peake Review*, Vol. 12 (Spring 1981), p. 16

104 'he told me that he was doing some drawings' from 'Mervyn Peake: A Pupil Remembers' by John Wood, *Mervyn Peake Review*, Vol. 12 (Spring 1981), p. 19

155 'Mr Pye is an agreeable confection' from a review of *Mr Pye* by Dominic Le Foe in the *Illustrated London News*, 1 November 1969

156 'They'd shoot you from below' from p. 70 of *Mr Pye* (in both Heinemann and Penguin editions)

157 Thorpe's tirade is from pp 198–200 of *Mr Pye* (Penguin edition, pp. 184–5)

161 'The finest examples' from Peake's introduction to his *Drawings*, p. 9

161 'in a sense, ugly of face' from *Titus Groan* (2nd edition), p. 51

169 'The dreadful and premature age' from *Titus Groan* (2nd edition), pp. 191–2

169 'Do not try and get solidity' from *The Craft of the Lead Pencil*, p. 5

170 'I have played too much' from *A World Away* by Maeve Gilmore, p. 128

177 'These, the imponderable platforms' from Peake's introduction to his *Drawings*, p. 7

192 'People now all seem' from a letter to Peake dated 10 February 1958

192 'For a moment they beamed' from *Mervyn Peake Review*, Vol. 23 (1990) [p. 10]

195 'To north, south, east or west' from *Titus Alone*, p. 7 (2nd edition, p. 9)

202 'You must take me there' from *Titus Alone*, p. 182

206 'The castle is a-float' from *Titus Alone*, p. 151

208 'Even as he spoke' from *Titus Alone* (2nd edition), p. 247

210 'It was at the private opening' from a letter written to G. Peter Winnington in October 1973; not previously published

Above
'We know what we know'

Select Bibliography

Fiction

Captain Slaughterboard Drops Anchor, Country Life, London, 1939

Gormenghast, Eyre and Spottiswoode, London, 1950 (2nd edition, 1968)

Letters from a Lost Uncle, Eyre and Spottiswoode, London, 1948

Titus Groan, Eyre and Spottiswoode, London, 1946 (2nd edition, 1968)

Titus Alone, Eyre and Spottiswoode, London, 1959 (2nd edition, 1970)

Mr Pye, Heinemann, London, 1953 (Penguin, Harmondsworth, 1972)

Poetry

A Book of Nonsense, Peter Owen, London, 1972

The Glassblowers, Eyre and Spottiswoode, London, 1950

Reverie of Bone, Bertram Rota, London, 1967

The Rhyme of the Flying Bomb, Dent, London, 1962

Rhymes Without Reason, Eyre and Spottiswoode, London, 1944

Selected Poems, Faber, London, 1972

Shapes and Sounds, Chatto and Windus, London, 1941

Non-Fiction

The Craft of the Lead Pencil, Allan Wingate, London, 1946

Compendiums

Drawings by Mervyn Peake, Grey Walls Press, London, dated 1949, published 1950

Drawings of Mervyn Peake, Davis-Poynter, London, 1974

Peake's Progress, Allen Lane, 1978 (corrected edition, Penguin, Harmondsworth, 1981)

Writings and Drawings, Academy, London, 1974

Illustrations

Anon, *Ride a Cock-Horse and Other Nursery Rhymes*, Chatto and Windus, London, 1941

Austin, Paul Britten, *The Wonderful Life and Adventures of Tom Thumb*, Radio Sweden, Stockholm, 1954 (Part 1) and 1955 (Part 2)

Balzac, Honoré de, *Droll Stories*, Folio Society, London, 1961

Carroll, Lewis, *Alice's Adventures in Wonderland* and *Through the Looking-Glass*, Zephyr Books, Stockholm, 1946 (2nd edition, Allan Wingate, London, 1954)

Carroll, Lewis, *The Hunting of the Snark*, Chatto and Windus, London, 1941

Coleridge, Samuel Taylor, *The Rime of the Ancient Mariner*, Chatto and Windus, London, 1943

Collis, Maurice, *Quest for Sita*, Faber and Faber, London, 1946

Crisp, Quentin, *All This and Bevin Too*, Nicholson and Watson, London, 1943

Dickens/Peake, *Sketches from Bleak House*, Methuen, London, 1983

Grimm, Brothers, *Household Tales*, Eyre and Spottiswoode, London, 1946

Haynes, Dorothy K., *Thou Shalt Not Suffer a Witch*, Methuen, London, 1949

Hole, Christina, *Witchcraft in England*, Batsford, London, 1945

Joad, C.E.M., *The Adventures of the Young Soldier in Search of the Better World*, Faber, London, 1943

Laing, Allan M. (compiler), *Prayers and Graces*, Gollancz, London, 1944

Stevenson, Robert Louis, *Dr Jekyll and Mr Hyde*, Folio Society, London, 1948

Stevenson, Robert Louis, *Treasure Island*, Eyre and Spottiswoode, London, 1949

Wilde, Oscar, *Mervyn Peake/Oscar Wilde*, Sidgwick and Jackson, London, 1980

Wyss, Johann R., *The Swiss Family Robinson*, Heirloom Library, London, 1949

Notes on Contributors

Sebastian Peake is the eldest of Mervyn Peake's and Maeve Gilmore's three children. For many years he worked in the wine trade but now spends much of his time giving illustrated talks on his father's life and work at literary festivals and other events across Europe and the USA. He is author of a memoir, *A Child of Bliss*, available from Vintage Books.

Alison Eldred ran the artists' agency Young Artists (now Arena) from 1976 to 2000 and continues to act as a consultant with the agency. She has considerable experience of working in the field of book illustration, especially in the area of science fiction and children's books.

G. Peter Winnington has been researching Mervyn Peake's life and work for more than thirty years. He has edited periodicals on Peake and revised the texts of the Titus books for Penguin. His biography of Mervyn Peake, *Vast Alchemies: The Life and Work of Mervyn Peake*, was published by Peter Owen in 2000, and he has a critical study coming out shortly from Liverpool University Press/Chicago University Press.

Michael Moorcock is a prolific writer, best known for his Elric novels, his 'Colonel Pyat' quartet and *Mother London*. He is the recipient of the World Fantasy Award, the Guardian Fiction Prize and Prix Utopiale, among other prizes. He was formerly editor of the highly respected literary magazine *New Worlds* and a personal friend of Mervyn Peake and his family.

Joanne Harris is the author of a number of highly praised novels, including the Whitbread Award-nominated *Chocolat*, now made into a successful feature film.

Chris Riddell is a cartoonist for the *Observer* newspaper and is well known for his collaboration with Paul Stewart on *The Edge Chronicles* as well as for his illustrations for the recent award-winning edition of *Gulliver's Travels*.

John Wood attended the Central School of Art and Crafts in the mid-1950s and was taught drawing by Mervyn Peake. He subsequently worked in film animation and publishing before turning freelance as a writer and artist. He is now retired.

John Howe has illustrated many books but is best known as the artist who painted Gandalf for the centenary edition cover of *The Lord of the Rings* and who worked with Peter Jackson and Alan Lee as concept artist on the Tolkien feature-film trilogy.

John Constable, playwright, poet and performer, has written a number of successful dramas and adapted the Titus trilogy as an acclaimed stage play in 1992.

David Glass, founder of the David Glass Ensemble in 1989, directed the 1992 stage adaptation *Gormenghast*.

Estelle Daniel trained as a theatre director and worked as a BBC script editor. She later worked as head of development for the BBC drama producer Michael Wearing and produced the much-admired 2000 television adaptation of *Gormenghast*.

Langdon Jones, musician and writer, worked on the original manuscripts of *Titus Alone* to produce the definitive edition published in 1970.